Intensive Reading Course on Chinese Culture: Contemporary China

中国文化精读教程：当代中国

冯薇薇 张超 编著

SinolinguA
华语教学出版社

First Edition 2025

ISBN 978-7-5138-2561-0

Published by Sinolingua Co., Ltd
24 Baiwanzhuang Street, Beijing 100037, China
Tel: (86)10-68320585, 68997826
Fax: (86)10-68997826, 68326333
http://www.sinolingua.com.cn
E-mail: hyjx@sinolingua.com.cn
Facebook: www.facebook.com/sinolingua
Printed by Beijing Hucais Culture Communication Co., Ltd

Printed in the People's Republic of China

前 言

《中国文化精读教程》是参照《国际中文教育中文水平等级标准》和《国际中文教育用中国文化和国情教学参考框架》（简称《参考框架》）的指导和要求开发而成的系列教程。本系列教程语言难度控制在《国际中文教育中文水平等级标准》中级的水平，文化理解的分级目标控制在《参考框架》中级阶段，可应用于海外各个国家中学到大学阶段，亦可与国际中文教育精读课程（中级）相结合。

本系列教程共三册，每个分册分别对应《参考框架》中级阶段的三大主题——社会生活、传统文化和当代中国，涵盖15个话题，设置30篇课文，覆盖80多个文化点，力求完成中级阶段所要求的教学内容和目标，即：了解中国社会生活、传统文化和当代中国国情的基本知识，比较中国文化和本土文化的主要异同，理解多样性。每篇课文的教学内容包括：课文阅读（附英文翻译）、短视频、生词表、语法点、结构分析、练习、文化教学活动。课文的词汇难度控制在4～6级之间，每篇课文包含约20个生词，3～5个成语或惯用语，1～3个语法点。

本系列教程选材兼具趣味性和讨论性。我们精心挑选了一系列文化趣事、社科美文、热点新闻，以及爆款视频的文本，确保课程内容丰富多元、动态活泼，力求在体现中华文化深厚底蕴的同时也能反映当下中国社会的热点话题。我们希望这些文章能够引领学生深入探索中国文化的内涵，发现文化差异，拓展视野，激发学生对中华文化和跨文化交际的热情与好奇心。本系列教程中还设计了丰富的文化探究活动和课堂讨论环节，旨在从多个角度、多个层面引导学生探索文化的奥秘，启发学生思考。

我们希望，通过学习本系列教程，学生不仅能够深入了解中华文化，更能够提升跨文化交际敏感度和能力，成为真正具有国际视野的人才。

目录

话题一 地理

教学内容和目标	文化点
1. 了解中国自然地理的概况和主要特点。 2. 了解中国行政区。 3. 理解中国环境保护面临的挑战和应对举措。	西高东低，母亲河，特别行政区，水资源保护，粤港澳大湾区

GRAND LISBOA

课文 1　中国的母亲河

课前热身

请仔细观察下面这张图片，用两分钟左右的时间描述一下你在图片上看到了什么，以及你对图片的理解。

课文 1

扫一扫，看视频

中国的母亲河

依水而行，傍水而生。千百年来，黄河滋养万物，恩泽一方，是华夏文明的主要发源地。

青海省贵德县素有“天下黄河贵德清”的美誉，却也曾有“守着黄河用不上水”的悲凉。在过去，黄河满足不了贵德百姓的日常生活用水，原因何在呢？

青海省海南藏族自治州贵德拉西瓦灌溉工程建设管理局局长李占彪说：“我们的耕地、老百姓居民区都在（海拔）2200 米以上，但是黄河都处在（海拔）2200 米以下，农田灌溉和老百姓吃水都需要提灌才能解决。”拉西瓦灌溉工程可以引黄河水直流灌溉农田，给老百姓减轻负担。

借黄河水之力，助黄河儿女民生，灌溉工程成为当地政府的头等大事。2023 年拉西瓦灌溉工程全面竣工通水后，灌溉面积达 20.02 万亩，解决 87 个行政村的灌溉问题，8 万余人因工程受益。

黄河水以无私的爱滋养一方百姓，复苏一片新绿。水养人，人亦养水。天人合一是自然界的盛世美景。四川省若尔盖县便有一处人间仙境，名为“花湖”。

若尔盖湿地国家级自然保护区管理局科研科科长索郎多尔吉说："黄河是我们中国的母亲河，我们这里的花湖其实是在给母亲河注入新鲜的血液。为了让母亲河不在上游断流，我们现在从国家层面、政府层面投入相当大的人力、财力保护这片湿地。我跟很多年轻的同事说，我们要像管自己家里一样把它管理好。"

"落霞与孤鹜齐飞，秋水共长天一色。"眼前这片花湖美景犹如世外桃源般让人如痴如醉，而相邻不远的西仓村仍行进在治沙还绿的征程上。

若尔盖县林草局生态修复助理工程师涂胜说："我第一次来的时候，这儿还是蛮荒凉的。这么走三公里看到的地方都是沙，没有一点点草。现在若尔盖的极重度沙化地基本上固定下来了，不会再有很大的蔓延。我们想的不是很伟大，就是想把自己县上的沙化治理好，让生态修复过来。黄河就是大家的母亲河，我们一定会帮她把伤口抚平的。"

Mother River of China

Follow the river waters and live by it. For thousands of years, the Yellow River has nurtured the Chinese civilization, leading it to prosperous glory.

Guide County in Qinghai Province is known as "having the purest water of the Yellow River". But sadly, with the Yellow River running through the land, its water couldn't be used for daily life in the past. Why was that?

Li Zhanbiao, Director of Guide Laxiwa Irrigation Project Construction and Management Bureau of Hainan Tibetan Autonomous Prefecture, Qinghai Province, said, “Our cultivated land and people’s residential areas are located 2,200 meters above sea level, but the Yellow River flows below that level. This poses problems regarding farmland irrigation and drinking water demand.” With the help of Laxiwa Irrigation Project, the Yellow River water can be channeled for farmland irrigation to relieve the public burden.

The Yellow River water can enhance people’s quality of life, so the irrigation project is a top priority of the local government. After the Laxiwa Irrigation Project was put into operation in 2023, the local irrigation area reached 133.47 square kilometers, solving the irrigation woes of 87 villages with more than 80,000 inhabitants.

With its selflessness, the Yellow River brings about a green landscape. Both mankind and water draw nourishment from each other. When nature and humans are in harmony, miracles happen. Ruoergai County, Sichuan Province is home to a fairyland called “Flower Lake”.

Solan Dorjee, Chief of the Scientific Research Section of Ruoergai Wetland National Nature Reserve Management Bureau, said, “The Yellow River is regarded as the ‘mother river’ in China. In fact, our Flower Lake is infusing fresh water into the mother river so that its waters are not cut off upstream. We are now investing considerable human and financial resources at the national and local government levels to protect this wetland. I told many of our young colleagues that we would manage it just as we manage our own homes.”

“Solitary ducks fly against the setting sun while the waters below mirror the hues of the sky above." The beautiful scenery of the Flower Lake resembles descriptions of a paradise. In its proximity, Xicang Village is still focusing on sand control and green restoration.

Tu Sheng, Assistant Engineer at the Ecological Restoration Unit of the Forest and Grass Bureau, Ruoergai County, said, "When I first came here, it was quite desolate. This way, three kilometers, you could only see sand and there was no grass. With our efforts, the threat of severe desertification in Ruoergai has been removed. We will take measures to control desertification in our county and restore the ecological environment. The Yellow River, our mother river, we will soothe all its wounds."

生词表

生词

1. 美誉	měiyù	good reputation
2. 悲凉	bēiliáng	desolation
3. 灌溉	guàngài	to irrigate
4. 耕地	gēngdì	arable land
5. 提灌	tíguàn	lift irrigation
6. 民生	mínshēng	people's livelihood
7. 受益	shòuyì	benefit from
8. 无私	wúsī	selfless
9. 滋养	zīyǎng	to nourish

10. 复苏	fùsū	to resuscitate
11. 湿地	shīdì	wetland
12. 征程	zhēngchéng	journey
13. 生态	shēngtài	ecology
14. 荒凉	huāngliáng	desolate
15. 蔓延	mànyán	to spread
16. 抚平	fǔpíng	to console

成语、俗语、惯用语等

1. 恩泽一方	ēnzé-yìfāng	favor bestowed (by a superior)
2. 天人合一	tiānrén-héyì	unity of man and nature
3. 人间仙境	rénjiān-xiānjìng	fairyland on earth
4. 世外桃源	shìwài-táoyuán	land of idyllic beauty
5. 如痴如醉	rúchī-rúzuì	intoxicating

语法点

却：表示转折的词语。

例句： 青海省贵德县素有“天下黄河贵德清”的美誉，却也曾有“守着黄河用不上水”的悲凉。

课文结构分析

请根据这个思维导图，用完整的句子对课文进行复述。

- 中国的母亲河
  - 黄河
    - 是华夏文明的主要发源地
  - 困难
    - 青海省贵德县
    - 县城：（海拔）2200 米以上
    - 黄河：（海拔）2200 米以下
    - 农业用水和生活用水需要提灌解决
  - 灌溉工程
    - 灌溉面积达 20.02 万亩
    - 解决了 87 个行政村的灌溉问题
    - 8 万余人受益
  - 守护黄河
    - 若尔盖花湖湿地国家级自然保护区
    - 西仓村治沙还绿工程

练习

1. 根据课文内容，将左边的词语和右边的解释搭配起来。（5 分）

（1）傍水而生	□	A. 农田
		B. 最重要的事情
（2）美誉	□	C. 好听的称呼
		D. 以海平面为起点的高度
（3）耕地	□	E. 在河水两岸生活
		F. 为了生活去抬水
（4）海拔	□	G. 大海
（5）头等大事	□	H. 美丽的样子

2. 根据课文内容回答下面的问题。（4分）

（1）花湖位于中国的哪个地方？

（2）花湖位于黄河的哪个部分？

（3）花湖的地理特征是怎么样的？

（4）“我们这里的花湖其实是在给母亲河注入新鲜的血液”，“新鲜的血液”指的是什么？

3. 用课文中的词语填空。（3分）

（1）如今，越来越多的青少年沉迷电脑到了__________的地步。

（2）地震过后，到处是一片__________的景象。

（3）传染病正在灾区__________。

4. 根据课文内容完成下列表格。（3分）

姓名	地区	负责的工作
李占彪	青海省海南藏族自治州贵德县	（1）
索朗多尔吉	（2）	若尔盖湿地国家级自然保护区管理
（3）	若尔盖县西仓村	治沙还绿

5. 上网找出中国河流分布地图，完成下面的表格。

中国河流分布

中国东部河流（七大水系）	中国西部河流（两大水系）	中国著名运河（两大运河）

课文 2　澳门

课前热身

请仔细观察下面这张图片，用两分钟左右的时间描述一下你在图片上看到了什么，以及你对图片的理解。

课文 2

扫一扫，看视频

澳　门

中国东南沿海的珠江三角洲有一座精美的城市——澳门。澳门虽小，却有着深厚的历史积淀。虽然总是把澳门与香港相提并论，但澳门却另有自己独特的城市魅力。

相传澳门得名于妈祖。16 世纪，葡萄牙人从妈阁庙附近登陆时问当地人这里的地名，因在妈阁庙旁，当地人便回答“妈阁”，于是澳门便以谐音被命名为 Macao。

独特的历史让澳门成为一座既古典又现代的中西合璧之城。澳门半岛上聚集了大三巴、炮台、玫瑰堂等文化景点，街道上狭窄的石子路、盘根错节的榕树、触手可及的斑驳墙壁、巴洛克式的雕花装饰，都藏着澳门诉不尽的故事。城市的另一边则是完全不同的画面——氹仔岛上坐落着一座座奢华的高级酒店，通宵不熄的娱乐场灯光、极其现代的购物商城都在向游客诠释着澳门的另外一面。

澳门回归祖国 20 多年来，经济实现跨越式发展。据澳门统计局公布的数字，本地生产总值从回归之初的 518.7 亿澳门元增加到 2020 年的 4346 亿澳门元；至 2020 年底，累计财政盈余达到 6500 亿澳门元，外汇储备超过 1900 亿澳门元，较 1999 年分别增长 193 倍和 6.2 倍，大大增强了抵御外部风险的能力。澳门进入历史上发展最好最快的时期，成为全球经济增速最快的地区之一。

20 多年来，澳门百姓安居乐业。经济多年持续的发展给澳门带来了高就业率、低失业率和居民收入水平的不断提高。澳门的失业率由 1999 年的 6.4% 降至 2018 年的 1.8%，近年一直维持在这一低水平。

20 多年来，澳门彰显多元文化魅力。在澳门，中华文化得到传承，多元文化得以发展，不只建筑中西合璧，还有和谐共存的宗教、族群。随着时代的发展进步，澳门还形成了绚丽迷人的节庆文化，“盛事之都”“美食之都”等成为新的亮丽名片。作为世界知名旅游目的地，澳门每年吸引入境旅客近 4000 万人次，让“居之者忘老、寓之者忘归、游之者忘倦”。

20 多年来，世界目睹了澳门翻天覆地的变化。今日的澳门已成为世界旅游休闲中心、中国与葡语国家商贸合作服务平台，相信澳门会稳步前行，持续繁荣。

Macao

Macao is a scenic city located on the Pearl River Delta on the southeast coast of China. Small though it is, Macao has a rich history and cultural heritage. Although it is often grouped with Hong Kong, Macao has its quaint charm.

Macao was thought to get its name from A-Ma Temple, a temple to the Chinese sea-goddess Mazu. In the 16th century, when the Portuguese landed near the A-Ma Temple and asked the place name, the local residents replied Maa-gok or A-maa-gok (literally meaning the Mother's Temple). Hence came the name of Macao.

Today, the city is classical and modern at the same time with a harmonious combination of Chinese and Western elements. You can enjoy cultural attractions on the Macao peninsula such as the Ruins of Saint Paul's, Mount Fortress, Macao Rose Hall, etc. You can feel the history on those narrow cobbled streets, old banyans with twisted roots and gnarled branches, mottled walls, and Baroque decorations. But on the other side of the city, on Ilha da Taipa, stand various grand, luxury hotels, brightly-lit entertainment centers, and modern shopping malls, telling you the modern story of Macao.

Macao has made great strides in economic development since its return to the motherland in 1999. According to the figures released by the Macao Bureau of Statistics, its gross domestic product increased from MOP 51.87 billion in 1999 to MOP 434.6 billion in 2020; by the end of 2020, the accumulated fiscal surplus reached MOP 650 billion, 193 times higher than that in 1999, and the foreign exchange reserve exceeded MOP 190 billion, 6.2 times higher than that in 1999. This has greatly enhanced Macao's ability to resist external risks. Macao has now entered a phase of speedy growth, becoming one of the fastest-growing regions in the world.

Over the past 20 years, local residents have lived and worked in peace and contentment. The continuous economic development over the years has led to a high employment rate and a spike in income. The unemployment rate dropped from 6.4% in 1999 to 1.8% in 2018 and has since remained at this level.

Macao offers its multicultural charm through its architecture blending Chinese and Western elements and the harmonious coexistence of religions and ethnic groups. As peace and prosperity reigns, Macao has developed various vibrant festivals, and successfully established its brands as a "City of Events" and a "Creative City of Gastronomy". As a world-famous tourist destination, Macao attracts nearly 40 million inbound tourists every year. It is said to be a place which helps you forget your age and fatigue and feel reluctant to leave once you're there.

The past two decades have witnessed great changes in Macao. Now it is a world center of tourism and leisure and a service platform for business cooperation between China and Portuguese-speaking countries. Looking to the future, Macao will continue to move forward and achieve sustainable growth.

生词表

生词

1. 精美	jīngměi	exquisite
2. 积淀	jīdiàn	accumulation
3. 登陆	dēnglù	to land
4. 谐音	xiéyīn	homophone
5. 半岛	bàndǎo	peninsula

6. 聚集	jùjí	to gather
7. 狭窄	xiázhǎi	narrow
8. 斑驳	bānbó	mottled
9. 奢华	shēhuá	luxurious
10. 诠释	quánshì	to explain
11. 生产总值	shēngchǎn zǒngzhí	GDP
12. 财政盈余	cáizhèng yíngyú	fiscal surplus
13. 外汇储备	wàihuì chǔbèi	foreign exchange reserves
14. 抵御	dǐyù	to resist
15. 维持	wéichí	to maintain
16. 彰显	zhāngxiǎn	to showcase
17. 亮丽	liànglì	beautiful

成语、俗语、惯用语等

1. 相提并论	xiāngtí-bìnglùn	mention in the same breath
2. 中西合璧	zhōngxī-hébì	combination of Chinese and Western styles
3. 盘根错节	pángēn-cuòjié	intricate, complicated
4. 触手可及	chùshǒu-kějí	within reach
5. 跨越式发展	kuàyuèshì fāzhǎn	leap-forward development
6. 安居乐业	ānjū-lèyè	live and work in peace and contentment
7. 和谐共存	héxié gòngcún	harmonious coexistence
8. 翻天覆地	fāntiān-fùdì	turn the world upside down

语法点

1. 虽……却……：转折句，指两个分句之间具有转折关系。

例句：澳门虽小，却有着深厚的历史积淀。

2. 于是：连接分句，表示承接关系，用在后面分句的开头。

例句：因在妈阁庙旁，当地人便回答“妈阁”，于是澳门便以谐音被命名为Macao。

3. 不只……还有……：连接词，表示更进一层的意思。

例句：在澳门，中华文化得到传承，多元文化得以发展，不只建筑中西合璧，还有和谐共存的宗教、族群。

课文结构分析

请根据这个思维导图，用完整的句子对课文进行复述。

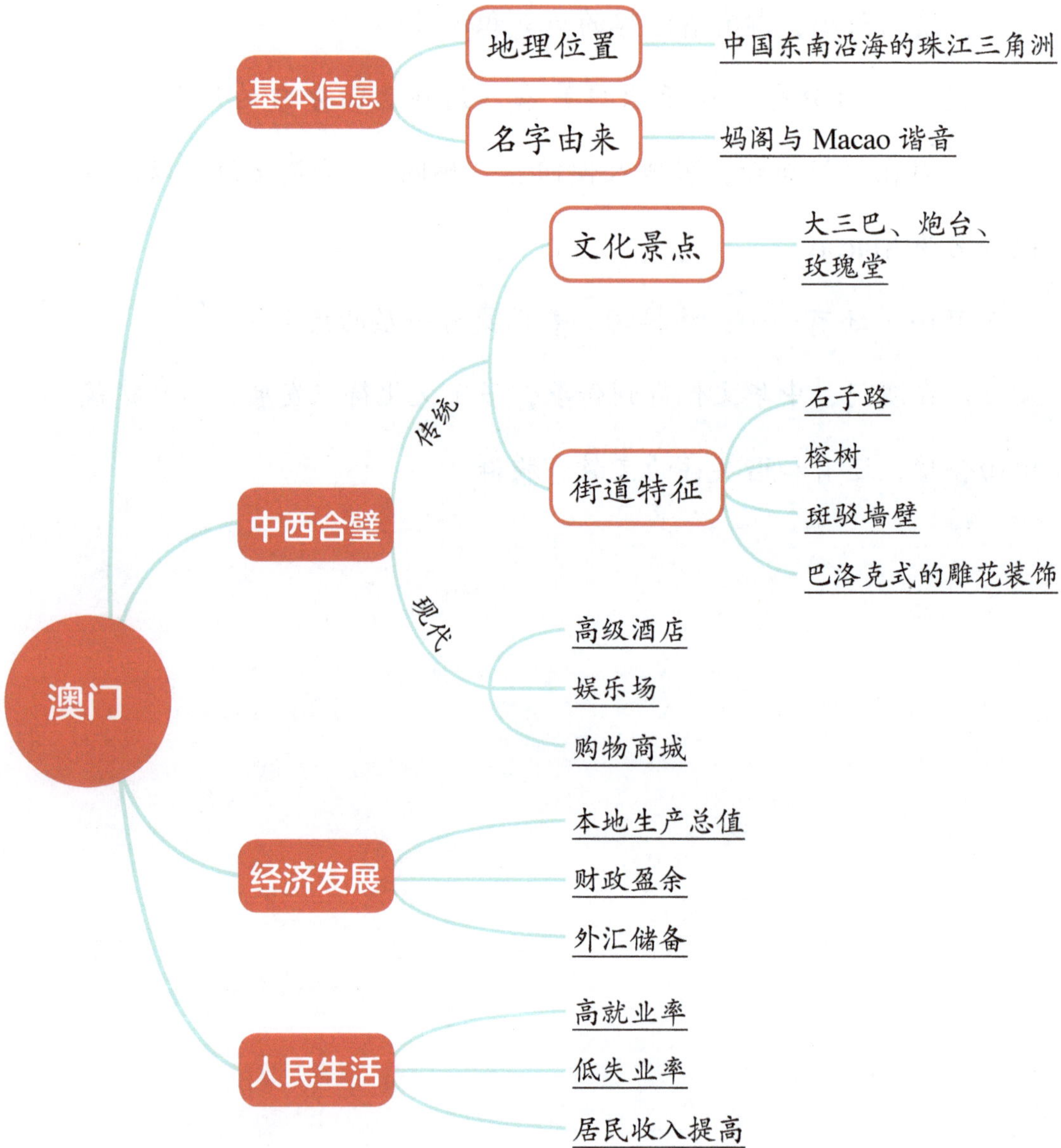

练习

1. 根据课文内容选择正确答案。（5 分）

（1）澳门和香港__________。 □

A. 一样

B. 不一样

C. 差不多

D. 不知道

（2）澳门的名字与什么有关？ □

A. 葡萄牙语发音

B. 妈祖的谐音

C. 登陆的街道名

D. 妈阁的发音

（3）澳门传统的一面表现为________。 □

A. 奢华的高级酒店

B. 现代化的购物商城

C. 巴洛克式的雕花装饰

D. 通宵不熄的娱乐场灯光

（4）下面哪一个不是澳门的景点？ □

A. 大三巴

B. 炮台

C. 山顶大佛

D. 玫瑰堂

（5）“游之者忘倦”的意思是什么？ □

A. 游泳的人忘了累

B. 来旅游的人不觉得累

C. 在街上游走的人觉得厌倦

D. 来游泳的人忘了疲倦

2. 根据课文内容，从右边选出最合适的结尾来完成左边的短句。（5 分）

（1）虽然人们总是把澳门与香港相提并论，☐

（2）独特的历史让澳门成为一座 ☐

（3）澳门成为全球经济 ☐

（4）澳门回归祖国 20 多年来，☐

（5）在澳门，不仅中华文化得到传承，☐

A. 百姓安居乐业。

B. 但澳门却另有自己独特的城市魅力。

C. 增速最快的地区之一。

D. 带来了澳门的高就业率。

E. 而且多元文化也得以发展。

F. 澳门还形成了绚丽迷人的节庆文化。

G. 为世界知名旅游目的地。

H. 既古典又现代的中西合璧之城。

3. 用课文中的词语填空。（5 分）

（1）他们两个人的成长背景不同，所以不能＿＿＿＿＿＿。

（2）香港是一个＿＿＿＿＿＿的城市。

（3）你要的东西＿＿＿＿＿＿，为什么还要我给你拿呢？

（4）香山公园犹如一幅＿＿＿＿＿＿的山水画。

（5）这几年，这座城市发生了＿＿＿＿＿＿的改变。

拓展练习

话题活动

1. 观看中央电视台的纪录片《澳门二十年》，直观地了解澳门回归祖国后的发展变化。

2. 上网查资料，每个小组负责查找有关澳门的某一方面资料，比如澳门的历史、经济支柱、景点、特色美食等，做成 PPT 在全班进行分享。

3. 假设你是一个澳门当地的导游，用你掌握的有关澳门的知识，向游客介绍澳门的历史、文化、景点等。

写作练习

即将大学毕业的你想以环保为主题，组织同学们完成一次为期五天的毕业旅行。请用 500 ～ 700 字写一篇演讲稿，说明本次旅行的形式和意义。你要在文章中提到：旅行的交通方式；景点的面貌；节假日景点的情况；旅游与环保的关系；旅游与景点保护的建议；旅行对青少年的影响。

文化点

粤港澳大湾区

粤港澳大湾区（Guangdong-Hong Kong-Macao Greater Bay Area）是由围绕中国珠江三角洲地区伶仃洋组成的城市群，包括广州、深圳、珠海、佛山、东莞、中山、江门、惠州、肇庆等九个城市，以及香港、澳门两个特别行政区。粤港澳大湾区的面积约为5.6万平方公里，截至2020年人口已超8600万，是中国国内生产总值（GDP）人均最高、经济实力最强的地区之一。

话题二 人口与民族

教学内容和目标	文化点
1. 了解中国各民族的概况和少数民族的习俗、风情。 2. 了解中国民族关系的特点和民族政策的落实。	少数民族，苗族，维吾尔族，少数民族风情，少数民族优惠政策

课文1　内蒙古科尔沁草原

课前热身

请仔细观察下面这张图片，用两分钟左右的时间描述一下你在图片上看到了什么，以及你对图片的理解。

课文 1

扫一扫，看视频

内蒙古科尔沁草原

中国的内蒙古自治区东北部有一片辽阔的草原。这里水草丰美，天地苍茫，牛羊信步，马儿嘶鸣，草原上的人世代在这片土地上繁衍生息。这里就是科尔沁草原。

蒙古语中"科尔沁"意为"弓箭手"，是蒙古族文化中勇敢和智慧的象征。科尔沁草原享有草原明珠的美誉。风吹草低见牛羊，这里辽阔的天空和壮美的草原也孕育出科尔沁儿女热情好客、乐观豁达的性格。

创作于20世纪50年代的歌曲《敖包相会》是几代中国人记忆中永恒的经典。"敖包"是最为知名的草原文化符号。蒙古语中"敖包"指的是人工堆成用作道路或地界标志的土石堆，以前的蒙古族人民把它当作神灵的住处来祭祀。"敖包"是蒙古族敬畏自然、热爱草原、感恩苍天的产物，是人与自然和谐共生的成果和象征。

每逢盛大节日，草原儿女都会穿上华丽的民族服装来到草原上祭祀敖包。人们围着敖包祈福，口中吟唱颂词，心中充满虔诚的祝福。头顶的天空和脚下的草原是他们的家园，敖包则是天地间最重要的坐标，也是他们精神世界最重要的坐标。人们通过祭祀敖包，将心中最纯粹、最美好的期盼向天地诉说。

安代舞是这片草原上世代传承的舞蹈形式，具有鲜明的民族风格和浓郁的生活气息，被称为“蒙古族第一舞”。在科尔沁地区，在喜庆丰收的日子里、在婚嫁和迎宾的宴会上，人们都要跳安代舞。甩巾踏步、拍手叉腰、向前冲跑等潇洒健美的动作，将人们心中的热情尽情释放，也将幸福和喜悦生动地传达给身边的人。

每年8月18日，科尔沁草原上都要举行赛马节，人们在这里娱乐、休息，享受赛马带来的快乐，分享丰收的喜悦。赛马体现的是草原儿女对于勇气和力量的推崇。著名的草原英雄嘎达梅林带领草原儿女英勇抗击强权、保卫家园的故事被写成英雄史诗世代传颂。

马头琴是草原上最常见的乐器，因以马为原型制作琴的头部而得名。马头琴琴声圆润饱满，低回宛转。每当琴声响起，草原上都好像会有一阵风吹起，吹过牛羊，吹过牧马，吹过敖包，也吹过草原牧民舞动的衣袖……

The Horqin Grassland in Inner Mongolia

There is a vast grassland in the northeast of China’s Inner Mongolia Autonomous Region. The prairie boasts abundant water and grass, vast heaven and earth with cattle and sheep walking and horses neighing. People on the grassland have lived on this land for generations. It is called the Horqin Grassland.

In Mongolian, "Horqin" means "people with bows and arrows", which symbolizes the bravery and wisdom of the ethnic group, and is hailed as the Pearl of Grassland. The vast sky and grassland also enables the Horqin people to have hospitable, optimistic, and open-minded character.

The song "Meet at the *Aobao*", written in the 1950s, is an eternal classic in the memory of several generations of Chinese people. *Aobao* has also become the symbol of grassland culture. In Mongolian, *Aobao* refers to the artificial pile of earth and stones used as a road sign or landmark, and, in the past, Mongolian people regarded it as the residence of the gods for worship. *Aobao* is the product of the grassland people's reverence for nature, love for the grassland and gratitude to the heaven, and is the epitome of the harmonious coexistence between man and nature!

Every grand festival, people with gorgeous costumes come to the grassland to offer sacrifices to *Aobao*. They gathered around *Aobao* to pray, chanting, full of piety. The sky above them and the grassland under their feet are their homes, and *Aobao* is the most important coordinate between heaven and earth, and also the most important coordinate of their soul world. By offering sacrifices to *Aobao*, people tell the purest and best expectations to heaven and earth.

Andai dance is a dance style inherited from generation to generation on this grassland. It has a distinct ethnic characteristic and a strong life atmosphere, and is known as the "the first dance of the Mongolian ethnic group". In the Horqin area, people perform this dance during harvest days, weddings, and welcoming banquets. Their passion for these events is conveyed through handsome acts like moving steps while swinging towels, clapping hands, arms around their waists, and running forward.

Every year on August 18, Horse Racing Festival is held on the Horqin Grassland, where people watch the horse racing and share their joy of harvest. Horse racing reflects the admiration of the grassland people for courage and strength. The grassland hero Gada Meiren led the people of the grasslands to fight bravely and defend their homes. His heroic stories were written as epic tales and passed down through generations.

The horsehead fiddle, a musical instrument often gracing the vast grasslands, derives its name from its striking likeness to a horse's noble visage. Its music resonates with mellowness and richness, both deep and sweet. Whenever its melodies fill the air, it seems to conjure a gust of wind sweeping across the open plains, caressing the grazing cattle and sheep, rustling the *Aobao* shrines, and setting the sleeves of grassland herders into a graceful dance.

生词表

生词

1. 信步	xìnbù	take a leisurely walk
2. 嘶鸣	sīmíng	to neigh

3. 豁达	huòdá	open-minded
4. 敬畏	jìngwèi	hold in awe and veneration
5. 虔诚	qiánchéng	pious
6. 健美	jiànměi	vigorous and graceful
7. 释放	shìfàng	to release
8. 推崇	tuīchóng	hold in esteem
9. 传颂	chuánsòng	be eulogized far and wide

语法点

被动句

被动句是指主语与谓语之间的关系是被动关系，主语是谓语动词所表示的行为的被动者、受事者，而不是主动者、实施者。

主语 + 被 / 叫 / 给 / 让 + 宾语 + 动词 + 其他成分

例句：（1）安代舞是这片草原上世代传承的舞蹈形式，具有鲜明的民族风格和浓郁的生活气息，被称为“蒙古族第一舞”。

（2）他的故事被写成英雄史诗世代传颂。

（3）我们被草原上的英雄事迹所打动。

（4）他被父亲叫到书房训斥了一番，最后苦着脸出来了。

课文结构分析

请根据这个思维导图，用完整的句子对课文进行复述。

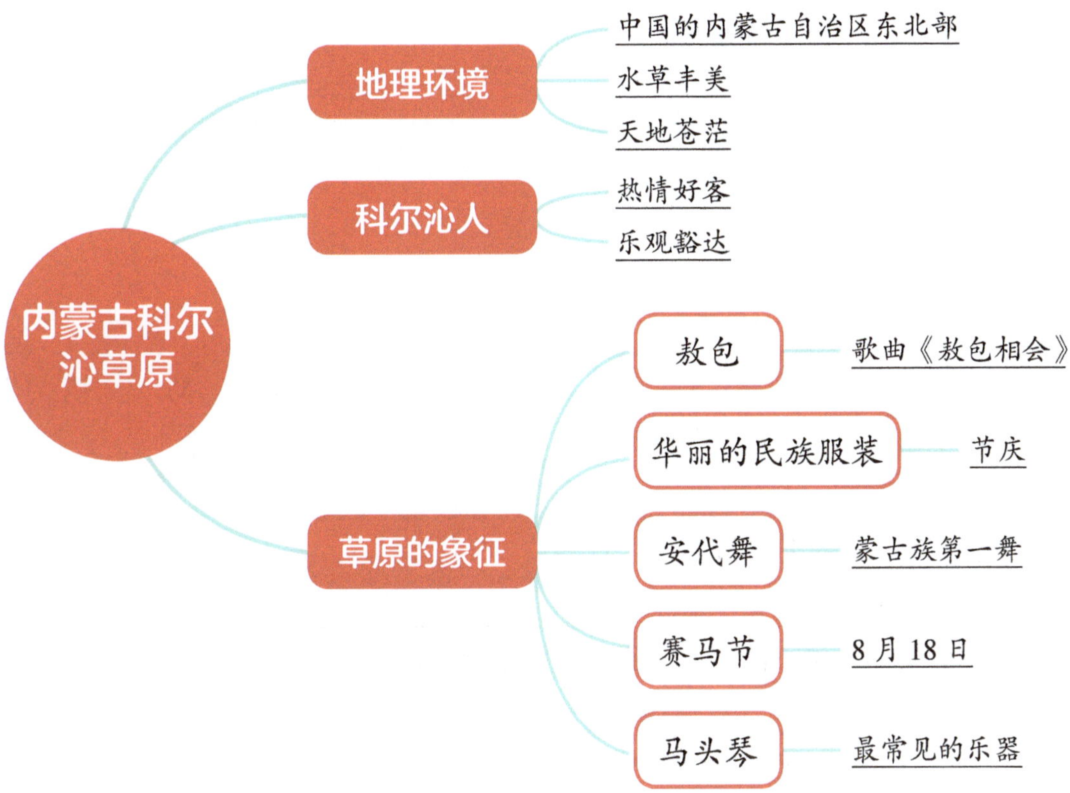

练习

1. 根据课文内容，选出五个正确的表述。（5 分）

☐ A. 科尔沁草原位于松辽平原东北部。

B. 科尔沁草原上有很多动物。

☐ C. 科尔沁是蒙古语，它的意思是带着弓箭的人。

D. 科尔沁草原有着深厚的文化传统和人文底蕴。

☐ E. 住在科尔沁草原上的人非常热情好客，也很乐观豁达。

□ F.《敖包相会》是19世纪50年代的歌曲。

G. 蒙古语中“敖包”指的是蒙古族住的蒙古包。

□ H. 以前的蒙古族人把敖包当作神灵的住处来祭祀。

2. 从课文里找出与下面各项意思最接近的词语。（5分）

（1）繁殖后代，以延续血脉 （　　）

（2）非常广阔 （　　）

（3）永远不变的 （　　）

（4）恭敬而真诚 （　　）

（5）把内含的能量放出来 （　　）

3. 根据课文内容判断下列说法的对错，并说明理由。（5分）

	对	错
（1）科尔沁草原上有牛有羊有马。	□	□
理由：________		
（2）科尔沁人非常热情好客、乐观豁达。	□	□
理由：________		
（3）草原上的人每天都穿上华丽的民族服装祭祀敖包。	□	□
理由：________		
（4）“蒙古族第一舞”只在喜庆丰收的日子里跳。	□	□
理由：________		
（5）马头琴是草原上不多见的一种民族乐器。	□	□
理由：________		

课文 2　新疆大巴扎

课前热身

请仔细观察下面这张图片，用两分钟左右的时间描述一下你在图片上看到了什么，以及你对图片的理解。

课文 2

扫一扫，看视频

新疆大巴扎

巴扎，维吾尔语，意为集市、农贸市场。从让人流口水的羊肉串到精致的手工乐器，再到华丽的皇家金制餐具，蓬勃发展的巴扎是那些淘宝人的一站式商店。但其实，那些从丝绸之路时期就保留下来的文化古韵才是巴扎最迷人的地方。

中国的新疆是古丝绸之路的重要节点，从古至今，往来东西方的商人在此汇聚，形成了繁荣的商业文明。早在公元前100多年，张骞出使西域到达新疆喀什时就曾有描述："这里有很热闹的街道和市场店铺，驼队马帮熙来攘往，杂货纷呈，穿着绚丽服饰的人们说着各种语言……"贸易的繁盛让原本以放牧为生的西部人转而从事农业和商业活动。很快，他们就成了丝路上最活跃的商人，巴扎也由此形成。

巴扎遍布新疆城乡，是这里最有人气的地方。每到巴扎日，附近方圆几十里的老百姓都会高高兴兴地前来"赶巴扎"。在这里，你能找到民族风情的毯子、金光闪闪的手工艺品、色彩斑斓的服饰……各种商品琳琅满目；美食更是应有尽有，羊肉串、手抓饭、烤包子、各式烤馕，定能让你大饱口福；最不能少的是新疆当地的水果——新疆日照充足，当地的水果果肉甘甜，晒制成的干果也别有一番风味，值得品尝。

让巴扎充满生命力的还有传统手工艺人。在这里，你会看到烧制土陶的老爷爷、抡着锤头千万次捶打的铜匠、手工制作传统乐器的少年……千年的技艺在这里代代相传，根深叶茂，完好地保留了下来。

巴托不仅是贸易场所，也是当地人交流情感的地方。维吾尔族人民好歌舞、爱热闹，常相聚在此谈天说地，消磨时光。熙熙攘攘的人潮与叫卖声、讨价声、欢笑声交汇在一起，形成一首独特的“新疆交响乐”，充满热腾腾的生活气息。今天，中国经济建设的发展给古老的巴扎注入了新活力。乌鲁木齐国际大巴扎、喀什大巴扎等成为展示当地历史、文化、民俗的窗口，是中外游客体验新疆风情的最佳去处。

如果你到了新疆，一定不要错过“赶巴扎”，会有惊喜哟！

Xinjiang Grand Bazaar

In the Uygur language, bazaar means market or trading place. From mouth-watering lamb kebabs to delicate handcrafted musical instruments to gorgeous royal gold tableware, the thriving bazaar is a one-stop shop for those treasure-hunters. But in fact, those ancient cultural charms that have been preserved since the Silk Road period are the most fascinating part of the bazaar.

Xinjiang in China is a hub of the ancient Silk Road. From ancient times to the present, merchants traveling between the East and the West have gathered here, forming a prosperous commercial civilization. As early as over a century BC, when Zhang Qian arrived in Kashgar, Xinjiang from the western regions, he described: "There are very busy streets and market shops, bustling camel caravans, groceries, people dressed in gorgeous clothes, speaking various languages..." The prosperity of trade made the local people, who originally made a living by grazing, turn to engaging in agriculture and industrial and commercial activities. Soon, they became the most active merchants on the Silk Road, and thus the bazaar was formed.

Bazaar scatters around Xinjiang and is the most popular place here. When Bazaar Day arrives, people from dozens of the miles away will joyfully participate in the "Bazaar Drive". Here, you can find all kinds of good things such as ethnic blankets, glittering handicrafts, and colorful clothes. Food is everything. Mutton kebabs, hand-grasped rice, baked stuffed buns, and a variety of baked naan will make for a delightful feast. If you come, you will never miss the local fruit. Since Xinjiang has sufficient sunshine, the fruit grown here is sweet, and the dried fruit has a unique flavor that is worth tasting.

Also keeping bazaar alive are traditional craftsmen. Here, you will see old men who made the clay, coppersmiths who swung hammers thousands of times, and teenagers who made traditional music instruments by hand. The handicraft skills formed over the past several thousand years have been passed down from generation to generation here.

In addition to trading, bazaar has become a place for locals to share their feelings, where the Uygur people get together to sing, dance, and chat to kill time. The bustling crowds, cries, bargaining, and laughter meet together, forming the most unique "Xinjiang Symphony". Today, the development of China has injected new vitality into the ancient bazaar. The Urumqi International Grand Bazaar and the Kashgar Grand Bazaar have become the showcase for local history, culture, and folk customs and are ideal places for tourists from home and abroad to experience regional customs.

If you come to Xinjiang, be sure to visit the enchanting bazaar!

生词表

生词

1. 蓬勃	péngbó	booming, thriving
2. 一站式	yízhànshì	one-stop
3. 古韵	gǔyùn	ancient charm
4. 节点	jiédiǎn	hub
5. 放牧	fàngmù	to graze
6. 人气	rénqì	popularity
7. 方圆	fāngyuán	surrounding area

成语、俗语、惯用语等

1. 熙来攘往	xīlái-rǎngwǎng	the hustle and bustle of large crowds
2. 琳琅满目	línláng-mǎnmù	a myriad of beautiful objects
3. 应有尽有	yīngyǒu-jìnyǒu	have everything that one expects to find
4. 大饱口福	dàbǎo-kǒufú	satisfy one's appetite by delicious food

5.	根深叶茂	gēnshēn-yèmào	have deep roots and luxuriant leaves—be well-established
6.	熙熙攘攘	xīxī-rǎngrǎng	streams of people busily coming and going

语法点

如果：假设复句。指分句之间具有假设关系的复句。前边的分句提出一句假设的情况，后面的主句说明在这种假设的情况之下所产生的结果。

例句：如果你到了新疆，一定不要错过“赶巴扎”，会有惊喜哟！

课文结构分析

请根据这个思维导图，用完整的句子对课文进行复述。

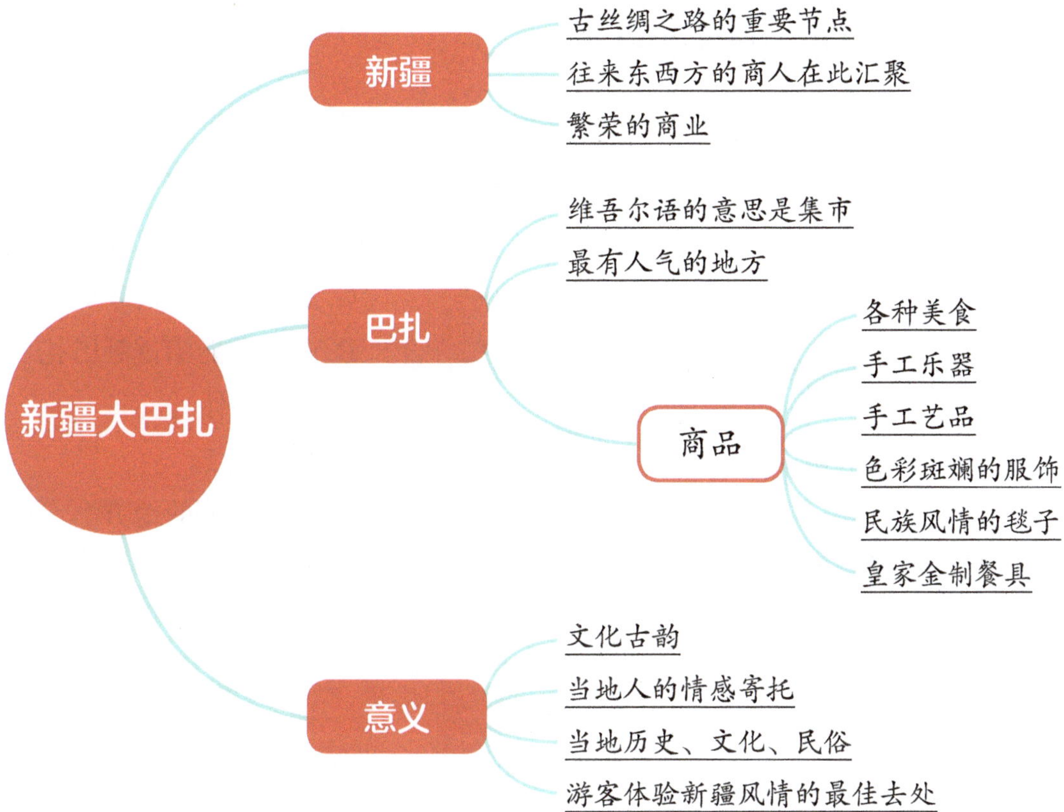

练习

1. 根据课文内容回答下面的问题。（5 分）

（1）在新疆的哪里可以找到巴扎？

（2）巴扎日会出现什么样的场景？

（3）为什么新疆的瓜果特别甜？

（4）为什么巴扎的生命力一直在延续？（2 分）

2. 从课文中找出与下面各项意思最接近的词语。（5 分）

（1）形容颜色灿烂的样子 ________

（2）形容眼前美好的东西很多 ________

（3）形容东西齐全 ________

（4）痛痛快快地吃一顿 ________

（5）根扎得深，枝叶就长得繁茂 ________

3. 根据课文内容，从右边选出最合适的结尾来完成左边的短句。（5 分）

（1）巴扎是当地 □

（2）从古至今，往来东西方的商人 □

（3）古时候，张骞出使西域到达 □

（4）很快，他们成了丝路上 □

（5）巴扎也是当地人的 □

A. 在新疆汇聚。

B. 最有人气的地方。

C. 最活跃的商人。

D. 一定不能错过赶巴扎。

E. 新疆喀什。

F. 重要节点。

G. 交流情感的地方。

H. 新疆交响乐。

拓展练习

话题活动

活动 A

观看《舌尖上的中国》第二季中的《新疆人的幸福美食生活》，直观地了解新疆的美食。

活动 B

假设你是一个旅行社的职员，要向世界各地的游客推广中国少数民族地区的旅游项目。请设计一个宣传海报，内容包括：这个地区的文化特色（包括风土人情和节庆活动）、著名景点、特色美食。

写作练习

试比较中国人的婚礼和你们国家的婚礼有什么异同，写一篇 500 ～ 700 字的文章给你的同学们讲解一下。

文化点

少数民族优惠政策

中国是统一的多民族国家。迄今为止，经中国政府确认的民族有56个，比如汉族、蒙古族、回族、藏族、维吾尔族、苗族、彝族、壮族、布依族、朝鲜族、满族、傣族，等等。其中汉族人口最多，占总人口的91.11%。由于汉族以外的55个民族相对汉族来说人口较少，所以习惯上被称为“少数民族”。

为促进少数民族和民族地区的发展，保障少数民族合法权益，中国政府制定了许多优惠政策。在政治方面，实行民族区域自治制度，加大少数民族地区改革开放力度，对少数民族地区实行优惠的财政政策。在文化艺术方面，保护和发展少数民族文化和民族文化遗产，尊重少数民族风俗习惯（包括宗教信仰自由），繁荣少数民族文化艺术和民族传统体育运动，保护和发展少数民族传统医药。在教育方面，鼓励使用和发展少数民族语言文字，支持和帮助少数民族地区发展教育。在经济方面，加强少数民族地区基础设施建设，促进基础产业发展，发展少数民族地区农牧业经济，鼓励少数民族地区发展贸易。

话题三 教育

教学内容和目标	文化点
1. 了解中国基础教育的概况和主要特点。 2. 了解中国基础教育阶段的学生培养目标。 3. 理解中国教育改革和创新的特点和未来方向。	九年义务教育，希望工程，远程教育，网课，慕课，中国高考

课文 1　中国版《放牛班的春天》

课前热身

请仔细观察下面这张图片，用两分钟左右的时间描述一下你在图片上看到了什么，以及你对图片的理解。

课文 1

扫一扫，看视频

中国版《放牛班的春天》

在法国电影《放牛班的春天》里，克莱门特·马修老师在“池塘底教养院”成立合唱团，用音乐打开学生们封闭的心灵。

相似的故事正在中国真实上演——支教老师王聿晦带领一支由山区孩子组成的艺术团登上了国际都市的舞台。虽然登台时孩子们的脚步还有点儿胆怯，但放声歌唱时，他们不仅把云南山歌唱得流畅动听，就连英语、德语歌曲也唱得十分自如。

谁能想到，就在两年前，这些来自云南偏远山区腾冲大塘村的孩子甚至连简谱都还不认识。虽然大塘小学的设施还不错，但教师人员不足，尤其缺少艺术教育方面的老师。王聿晦毕业于中国名牌大学，从小学习音乐。来支教前她就计划在小学里组建艺术团，可是这个过程却比她想象的困难得多——没有音乐教室，没有乐器，学生们的乐理知识为零……王聿晦想办法买来竖笛、钢琴等乐器，孩子们学得很起劲儿。王聿晦忙得团团转，但她说，每次琴声停止与学生相视而笑的时候是她最幸福的瞬间。

艺术教育是为了激发人们对美和善的追求。音乐对孩子们的改变显而易见。在王老师的课上，一个曾经内向的小姑娘变得热情开朗，一个不合群的小男生开始懂得为他人考虑——就像电影里的情节一样，少年们开始用自己的实力来赢得尊重。

王琎琦想让孩子们走出大山去看看外面的世界，于是她在网上发起众筹，想办一个专场音乐会，没想到在30小时之内就筹到了10万余元。人们的爱心帮助山里娃圆了梦。

现在，越来越多的中国青年投身公益，他们尤其关注儿童与教育问题。在中国，人们常常将孩子比喻成花朵，把老师比喻成园丁。王琎琦曾说："音乐是洒向这个世界的蒲公英。"在电影《放牛班的春天》里，皮埃尔最终成为了音乐家，也许大塘小学的孩子中也会有人像他一样。但这不是最重要的，重要的是蒲公英的种子已经随风飘散，在更广阔的世界中发芽、生长。

Chinese Version of *The Chorus*

In the French film *Les Choristes* (*The Chorus*), a teacher named Clement Matthieu set up a choir in the Bottom of the Pond boarding school to open the students' closed hearts with music.

Similar stories are taking place in China. A volunteer teacher Wang Jinmei led an art troupe composed of children from mountainous areas to perform on the stage of an international city. They were a little bit timid as they stepped on the stage. But when they sang aloud, they sang the Yunnan folk song smoothly and the English and German songs very freely.

Who would have thought that these children didn't even know

musical notation just two years ago? They came from a remote region named Datang Village in Tengchong, Yunnan Province. Datang Primary School had good facilities but lacked teachers, especially those in art education. Wang graduated from a famous Chinese university and began to study music during childhood. Before becoming a volunteer teacher, she had planned to set up an art troupe in a primary school. Still, the process was much more difficult than she imagined—no music room, instruments or basic music knowledge among students here. Wang managed to buy such musical instruments as clarinets and a piano for them. The children showed keen interest in learning, and Ms. Wang was fully occupied. But she said that exchanging smiles with her students at the end of the piano sound was the most joyful moment.

Art education is a discipline with the aim to encourage people to pursue beauty and kindness. Music changed the children, obviously. Ms. Wang's class turned an introverted girl into an enthusiastic and cheerful one and an unsociable boy into one who cared for others—just like the plot in the movie. The teenagers began to use their own strength to win respect.

Wang hoped the children would venture out of the mountains to see the outside world, so she launched a crowdfunding campaign online to host a special concert. More than 100,000 yuan was raised within 30 hours, exceeding expectations. People's love helped these children realize their dreams.

Nowadays, an increasing number of young Chinese people are dedicating themselves to public welfare, particularly issues related to the children and education. In China, children are often compared to flowers and teachers to gardeners. Wang once said, "Music is the dandelions I spread to the world." In the movie *Les Choristes*, Pierre eventually became a musician, and maybe some of the children at Datang Primary School would be like him. But this is not the most important thing. What is important is that the dandelion seeds have been scattered in the wind, sprouting and growing in the wider world.

生词表

生词

1. 教养院	jiàoyǎngyuàn	reformatory
2. 胆怯	dǎnqiè	timid
3. 流畅	liúchàng	easy and smooth
4. 简谱	jiǎnpǔ	numbered musical notation
5. 竖笛	shùdí	clarinet
6. 瞬间	shùnjiān	fleeting moment
7. 开朗	kāilǎng	open and frank, optimistic
8. 合群	héqún	getting on well with others
9. 众筹	zhòngchóu	crowdfunding
10. 公益	gōngyì	public welfare
11. 比喻	bǐyù	be likened to
12. 园丁	yuándīng	gardener
13. 蒲公英	púgōngyīng	dandelion

成语、俗语、惯用语等

显而易见	xiǎn'éryìjiàn	obviously

语法点

1. 连……也：强调某些令人惊讶的信息。

例句： 他们不仅把云南山歌唱得流畅动听，就连英语、德语歌曲也唱得十分自如。

2. 甚至：连词，强调突出的事例（有更进一层的意思）。

例句： 这些孩子甚至连简谱都还不认识。

课文结构分析

请根据这个思维导图，用完整的句子对课文进行复述。

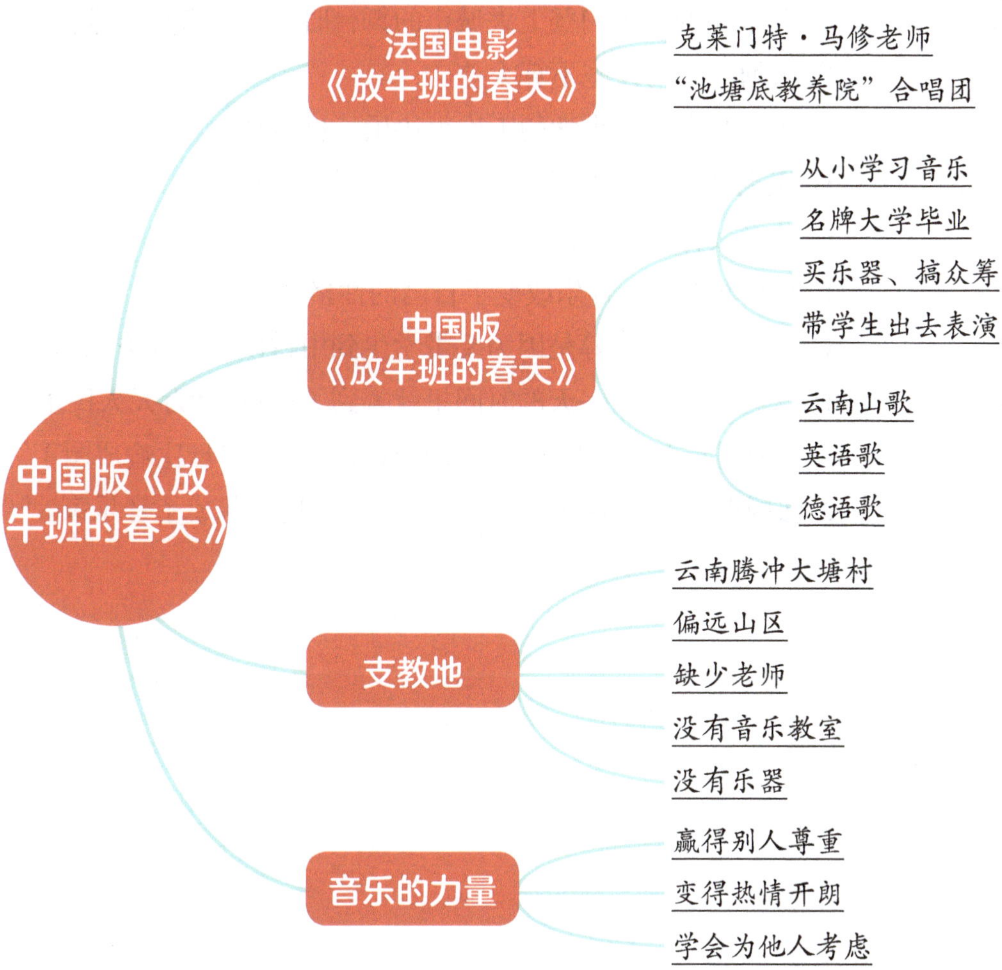

练习

1. 根据课文内容回答下面的问题。（8 分）

（1）电影《放牛班的春天》里，马修老师在教养院成立了什么样的艺术团体？

（2）大塘小学合唱团的学生可以用哪几种语言唱歌？（3 分）

（3）王老师为什么想举办一场音乐会？

（4）大塘小学的王老师的教育背景和爱好是什么？（2分）

（5）大塘小学的学生在王老师到来之前对音乐的了解有多少？

2. 根据课文内容，从下面的句子中找出正确的说法。（7分）

□ □ □ □ □ □ □

A. 艺术团的孩子们登上大城市的舞台时，心里有点儿害怕。

B. 大塘小学的设施不算太差。

C. 王老师在大塘小学的工作很快乐，也很轻松。

D. 王老师看着学生们开心地表演，感到非常幸福。

E. 艺术教育使人向善。

F. 有些学生因为音乐改变了自己的性格和品行。

G. 王老师发起众筹是因为要带学生到山村以外的地方去演出。

H. 王老师在不到一天的时间里就筹到了超过10万元人民币。

I. 在中国，人们喜欢把孩子比喻成花朵，把父母比喻成园丁。

J. 法国电影《放牛班的春天》的结局是皮埃尔成了音乐家。

课文 2　大山里的网络直播课

课前热身

请仔细观察下面这张图片，用两分钟左右的时间描述一下你在图片上看到了什么，以及你对图片的理解。

课文 2

扫一扫，看视频

大山里的网络直播课

中国甘肃省的山区有一所鹿马岔小学。这里一共只有三名学生，因为村里条件稍好的家长都会把孩子送去外地上更好的学校。这三个孩子都是家境比较贫困的。

幸运的是，时下中国年轻人中最火的社交方式——网络直播走进了他们的教室。一根网线、一台多媒体一体机、一个摄像头组成了鹿马岔小学的视频直播课堂。线上，一名音乐老师在屏幕上教孩子们乐谱，随时点名邀请学生演唱，并进行指导。线下，教室里还有一名助教老师负责组织管理课堂。

在甘肃省，像鹿马岔小学这样只有五名以下学生的学校有近千所。为了让这些贫困的孩子们接受更好的教育，从 2017 年开始，甘肃省开始了网络直播教学的试点。现在，鹿马岔小学所在区域内所有的学校都采用统一课表，聘请优秀的教师在线上直播教学，老师们可以通过视频切换跟各教学点的学生互动。网络直播将这些农村孩子联系起来，有的性格活泼、多才多艺的学生还成为了他们中的“小网红”。

中国互联网的迅猛发展为农村的教育事业带来了变化。新的互联网教育企业不断涌现、农村地区宽带建设加快，使得边远地区的学校能够享受到更多的公共服务和科技成果。中国政府从中发挥了巨大的推动作用。促进教育公平是中国政府最看重的民生问题之一，因为它是社会公平的重要基础。中国在 2014 年实现了九年义务教育全覆盖，而今鹿马岔小学通过网络直播让贫困学生学习以前接触不到的艺术课程，则体现了政府在教育公平方面有了更高的追求。

近年来，中国在互联网、人工智能等领域的巨大进展引起全球关注。我们可以看到，中国在谋求发展的同时，也在重视社会公平，努力让其发展成果为每个百姓所共享。有些改变或许需要时间，但是却在实实在在地发生着。

Online Courses Benefit Children in Poor Areas

There are only three students at Lumacha Primary School, which is located in a remote mountainous area in northwest China's Gansu Province. The children from the more affluent families in the community have been sent to better-equipped schools. The families of the three remaining students are not well-off.

Fortunately, live streaming, the trendiest social activity among the youth of China, is transforming the classes in Lumacha. The three students can take online courses with only an internet cable, an overhead projector, and a webcam. A music teacher appears on the screen and provides them with instructions on how to read musical notations, asks them to sing, and corrects their singing. A teaching assistant is also present in the classroom to manage the students.

Gansu has nearly 1,000 schools like Lumacha with less than five students. In order to provide better education to these children, the provincial authorities launched a pilot online education project in 2017. Now, all the schools in the area where Lumacha Primary School is located have adopted the same class schedule and recruited excellent teachers to give online courses. Online teachers can monitor and interact with students in different schools by video switching. Live streaming has connected children in rural areas. Some outgoing and versatile students have even become "online celebrities".

The rapid development of China's internet has brought changes to education in rural areas. Broadband construction in rural areas has been accelerating, and online education businesses have sprung up so that the schools in remote areas can have access to better public services and technologies. This should be attributed to the Chinese government's great role in pushing forward these projects. Promoting educational equity is one of the greatest concerns of the Chinese government because it is an important basis for achieving social fairness. Nine-year compulsory education had been implemented across the country by 2014. Now, through live online broadcasts, the students in Lumacha Primary School can access arts curricula that were unimaginable in the past, which is evidence to show China's greater pursuit of educational equity.

China's recent progress in internet technology and artificial intelligence has attracted global attention. While pursuing economic growth, the Chinese government is committed to promoting social fairness, enabling everyone to share in its development fruit. Some changes may take time, but they are on the way.

生词表

生词

1. 网络直播	wǎngluò zhíbō	live video streaming
2. 网线	wǎngxiàn	network cable
3. 多媒体一体机	duōméitǐ yìtǐjī	multimedia all-in-one machine
4. 摄像头	shèxiàngtóu	video camera
5. 聘请	pìnqǐng	to engage, to hire
6. 多才多艺	duōcái-duōyì	versatile
7. 迅猛	xùnměng	rapid
8. 宽带	kuāndài	broadband
9. 谋求	móuqiú	to pursue

语法点

1. 则：表示对比的连词。

例句： 中国在2014年实现了九年义务教育全覆盖，而今鹿马岔小学通过网络直播让贫困学生学习以前接触不到的艺术课程，则体现了政府在教育公平方面有了更高的追求。

2. 同时：连词，表示并列关系，常含有进一层的意味。

例句： 中国在谋求发展的同时，也在重视社会公平。

3. 使得：动词，（意图、计划、事物）引起一定的结果。

例句： 新的互联网教育企业不断出现、农村地区宽带建设加快，使得边远地区的学校能够享受到更多的公共服务和科技成果。

课文结构分析

请根据这个思维导图，用完整的句子对课文进行复述。

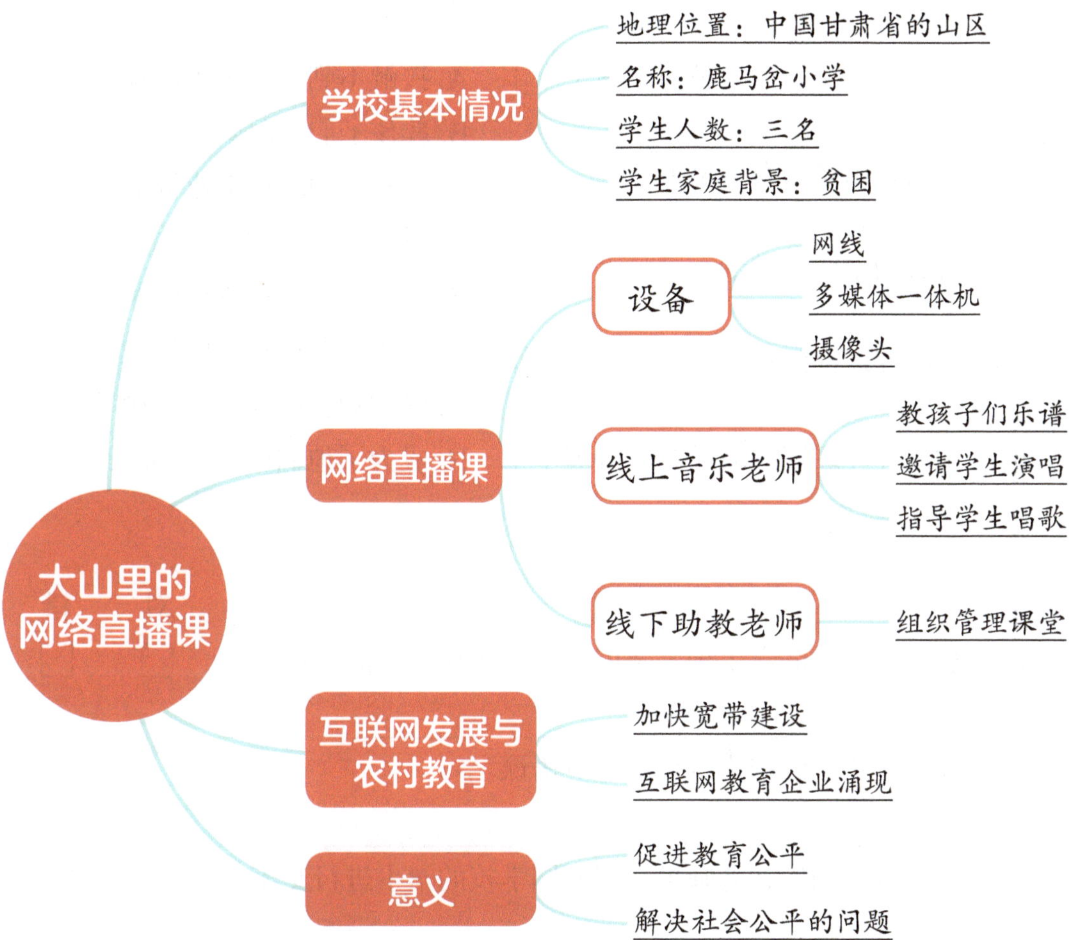

练习

1. 根据课文内容回答下面的问题。（5 分）

（1）鹿马岔小学的三名学生为什么继续留在这个学校？

（2）文中提到的音乐课是通过什么方式进行的？

（3）甘肃省有多少所学生不到五人的学校？

（4）鹿马岔小学所在区域内的所有学生都可以一起上网课吗？为什么？（两个都答对才可以得到 1 分）

（5）中国政府最看重的一个民生问题是什么？

2. 根据课文内容，从右边选出最合适的结尾来完成左边的短句。（5 分）

（1）村里条件稍好的家长会把孩子 □

（2）一名音乐老师在屏幕上 □

（3）所有的学校都聘请 □

（4）中国互联网的迅猛发展 □

（5）中国在互联网领域的巨大进展 □

A. 接触不到的艺术类课程。
B. 教孩子们学习乐谱。
C. 为农村的教育事业带来了变化。
D. 引起全球关注。
E. 更好的公共服务和技术
F. 送去外地上更好的学校。
G. 优秀的教师在线上直播教学。
H. 成为了他们中的“小网红”。

3. 根据课文内容判断下列说法的对错，并说明理由。（5 分）

	对	错
（1）鹿马岔小学的学生少，是因为学校所在地区的人口少。	□	□
理由：________		
（2）鹿马岔小学的网络直播课是英语课。	□	□
理由：________		
（3）通过视频切换，老师可以跟不同学校的学生进行交流。	□	□
理由：________		
（4）教育公平是社会公平的重要基础。	□	□
理由：________		
（5）鹿马岔小学的学生从小就接受艺术教育。	□	□
理由：________		

拓展练习

话题活动

观看电影《茶啊二中》，理解如何平衡传统应试教育模式和学生个性化发展之间的关系。

话题讨论

和同学分享一句座右铭或名人名言，说说它是怎么激励你的。

写作练习

有不少学生看到很多网红利用直播和短视频赚到了钱，便觉得高考和学业并没有那么重要，甚至有了退学当网红的想法。请你用 500 ～ 700 字写一篇文章来反驳这种现象和观点。

文化点

中国高考

普通高等学校招生全国统一考试，简称“高考”。它是中国重要的全国性考试之一，是由普通高中毕业生和具有同等学力的考生参加的选拔性考试。中国有1300多年科举考试的历史。1905年，清朝政府出于发展新教育、培养实用人才的需要，废除了科举制度，转而引进西方的学校考试制度。中国现代高考制度的建立就有了这样两个重要来源：一是科举考试制度所形成的传统考试思维和价值；二是西方现代考试制度的模式和手段。中国高考制度近些年进行了多次改革，包括取消文理分科、学生可以根据自己的特长和兴趣选择考试科目等。改革的意义在于：一是科学选拔人才；二是促进学生健康发展；三是维护社会公平。

话题四 科技

教学内容和目标	文化点
1. 了解中国当代科技的发展和最新成果。 2. 理解科技发展对中国经济和社会生活的影响。	5G 通信，科教兴国，科技人才引进和培养

课文1 “云游”中国

课前热身

请仔细观察下面这张图片，用两分钟左右的时间描述一下你在图片上看到了什么，以及你对图片的理解。

课文 1

扫一扫，看视频

云游中国

清明前后正是春游踏青的大好时节。以前的“云旅游”往往在朋友圈进行，现在随着技术的发展，旅游直播这种人在家中坐、身心“逛”世界的新旅行方式正受到人们的青睐。

博物馆“云课堂”

2020年，抖音短视频平台联合中国国家博物馆、敦煌研究院等九家博物院馆推出了“在家云游博物馆”活动。观众在观看直播云游博物馆的过程中，除了能够听到专业、有趣、生动的讲解外，还可通过线上直播平台与讲解员进行互动交流。这种形式让观众既欣赏了文物，又增长了见识，可谓一举两得。

布达拉宫“云探秘”

2020年3月1日，已有1300多年历史的布达拉宫完成了它的第一次直播。据了解，为了准备此次直播，政府部门专门准备了5G信号车。由于网络直播没有线下客流量的压力，本次直播还展示了一些极少开放的区域，比如以往游客去不了的金顶，在直播中可以近距离地看到。很多网友评论“这个直播太珍贵了”，还刷起弹幕来进行交流互动。

武汉大学“云赏樱”

为了让游客如约看上每年3月校园盛开的樱花，武汉大学特别开通了“云赏樱”通道。伴随着音乐，武汉大学樱花大道各个角度的画面来回切换，网友不停评论留言：“曾经多想拍拍没有人的樱花大道，现在只怀念全是人的樱花大道。”

随着5G时代的到来，以及中国在VR、AR等技术领域的快速发展，“云旅游”作为旅游的一种延伸，未来将与景区的线下旅游有机结合，比如在制订旅游计划前可以先在线上“身临其境”。这个环节说不定会成为以后出游的一项必备功课。

Virtual Touring to China

The coming of the Tomb-Sweeping Day, which usually falls in early April, also heralds the popularity of spring outings. Other than enjoying the beautiful pictures shared on social media, people can now access more immersive online travel experiences at home thanks to emerging live streaming platforms.

Online Classes on Museums

In 2020, nine popular museums, including the National Museum of China and the Dunhuang Academy of China, rolled out virtual tours via partnership with TikTok, a video-sharing platform. During the virtual tours, the online visitors can enjoy professional and engaging introduction and interact with guides in real-time. Such practices enable people to appreciate antiques in a more informative manner.

Online Visit to the Potala Palace

The Potala Palace, a landmark in southwest China's Xizang Autonomous Region, held a livestreaming tour session on March 1, 2020, the first time in its over 1,300-year history. 5G signal vehicles were in place to ensure smooth livestreaming, while some exhibition zones that are rarely open to the public, such as the golden roofs of the palace, were unveiled during the online tour. The digital tour impressed many online visitors and they exchanged their ideas on the bullet screen, which showed viewers' real-time comments and messages.

Online Viewing Cherry Blossoms in Wuhan University

Besides its academic fame, Wuhan University is also known for its cherry blossoms of March in spring. The university has set up an online platform for visitors to enjoy these blossoms from different angles while listening to music. Some visitors even joked that they used to desire for an empty cherry blossom venue on the campus, but now they miss the crowded one.

With the advent of the 5G era and China's rapid development in VR, AR, and other technologies, online tourism, a new extension of the industry, will be combined with offline tourism in scenic spots in the near future. For example, one can tour the destination online before making travel plans, which may become indispensable for future travel.

生词表

生词

1. 云游	yúnyóu	tour online
2. 短视频	duǎn shìpín	short video
3. 讲解	jiǎngjiě	to explain
4. 互动交流	hùdòng jiāoliú	to interact
5. 文物	wénwù	cultural relic
6. 见识	jiànshi	experience
7. 弹幕	dànmù	bullet comments
8. 如约	rúyuē	according to appointment
9. 樱花	yīnghuā	cherry blossom
10. 来回切换	láihuí qiēhuàn	switch back and forth

成语、俗语、惯用语等

1. 春游踏青	chūnyóu tàqīng	spring outing
2. 一举两得	yìjǔ-liǎngdé	gain two ends at once
3. 身临其境	shēnlínqíjìng	be personally on the scene

语法点

为了……：表示行为的目的。

例句：为了准备此次直播，政府部门专门准备了5G信号车。

课文结构分析

请根据这个思维导图，用完整的句子对课文进行复述。

- “云游”中国
  - 第一段
    - 新的旅行方式
      - 人在家中坐，身心“逛”世界
  - 第二段
    - 博物馆“云课堂”
      - 九家博物院馆
      - 听到专业、有趣、生动的讲解
      - 与讲解员进行互动交流
  - 第三段
    - 布达拉宫“云探秘”
      - 5G信号车
      - 展示一些极少开放的区域
      - 刷弹幕进行交流互动
  - 第四段
    - 武汉大学“云赏樱”
      - 各个角度的画面来回切换
      - 网友评论留言
  - 第五段
    - 5G、VR、AR技术发展
    - “云旅游”成为旅游的一种延伸
    - 与景区的线下旅游有机结合

练习

1. 根据课文内容回答下面的问题。（5 分）

（1）课文中哪句话解释了什么是“云旅游”？（1 分）

（2）“云游博物馆”活动可以让人“游览”多少家博物馆？（1 分）

（3）“一举两得”指的是什么？（2 分）

（4）“云游”布达拉宫时，可以看到哪些线下无法看到的景观？（1 分）

2. 根据课文内容判断下列说法的对错，并写出理由。（5 分）

	对	错
（1）每年的夏天是旅游踏青的大好时光。	□	□
理由：________		
（2）“云游”博物馆的时候可以向讲解员问问题。	□	□
理由：________		
（3）“云赏樱”的时候，游客可以看到日本的樱花。	□	□
理由：________		
（4）游客可以边听音乐边“云赏樱”。	□	□
理由：________		
（5）将来，人们既可以线下旅游，也可以“云旅游”。	□	□
理由：________		

3. 将左边的词语和右边的解释搭配起来。（5 分）

（1）踏青	□	A. 脚踩
		B. 郊游
（2）青睐	□	C. 亲自来到某个地方
（3）延伸	□	D. 喜爱
		E. 学校作业
（4）身临其境	□	F. 延展伸长
（5）必备功课	□	G. 必须要做的作业

课文 2　冰立方

课前热身

请仔细观察下面这张图片，用两分钟左右的时间描述一下你在图片上看到了什么，以及你对图片的理解。

课文 2

扫一扫，看视频

冰立方

伴随着阵阵呐喊声，几名队员卖力地用冰刷擦拭着冰面，一只精致的石壶在洁白的冰面上缓慢滑行着。北京冬奥会冰壶场馆“冰立方”内，一场民众冰壶体验赛正在进行。环顾四周，这个场馆可不仅仅是一个冰壶场馆那么简单。冰立方由 2008 年北京奥运会主游泳馆“水立方”改造而成，是一座可拆卸的、可临时进行“冰水转换”的场馆。

水立方曾在 2008 年的北京奥运会上大放异彩，见证了各国运动员的荣光。奥运会后，水立方社会化运营十分成功，成为奥运场馆赛后利用的典范。2015 年，北京成功申办 2022 冬奥会后，有人提出了一个大胆设想：让水和冰自由转换，可以使这个场馆更大限度地再利用，赛后也可以为民众提供更丰富的文化体育服务，改造后的冰立方将成为双奥之城的一个重要遗产。

那么，“水立方”是如何成为“冰立方”的呢？需要注意的是，冰壶对场地的要求是所有冰上项目中最为严苛的，如何保证可拆卸装置的稳固性是最大难题。在经过反复设计测算与试验后，设计团队最终将误差控制在了 2 毫米内。按照“冰立方”可拆卸的设计，冰面厚度设为 8 厘米，需要反复浇筑四五十层，耗时一周时间才能最终制成。

冰非常“敏感”，冰壶场馆要求空气不能流动，阳光不能直射，不能有多余的热辐射投到冰上。为此，设计团队将馆内的环境温度、湿度、光照系统，甚至声学系统都进行了智能化改造。

经过改造的冰立方春夏秋三季为水，冬季上冰，冬奥会后用于群众冰上运动培训和体验，助力实现“三亿人上冰雪”的目标。

百年的现代奥运历史留下了不少经典的场馆建筑，它们不仅是人类工程建筑的杰作，更是一座座体现现代奥林匹克精神的丰碑。然而，历届奥运会也都面临着奥运场馆赛后发展的难题。为了解决这一难题，设计师们在探索中寻求变革，例如：1992 年巴塞罗那奥运会的奥运村及场馆经过改造后成为游客打卡地；2012 年伦敦奥运会的许多场馆都是租赁建材、临时搭建，而主场馆“伦敦碗”则采用了乐高式的模块化建造法，赛后改建租给了西汉姆联队作为主场。在北京，从 2008 年夏季奥运会到 2022 年冬季奥运会，从水立方到冰立方，中国将可持续发展的理念引入奥运场馆的建设当中，探索奥运场馆的综合利用、持久利用的新模式，为现代奥林匹克运动的发展提供了“中国经验”。

The Ice Cube

Accompanied by bursts of shouts, several team members are working hard to sweep the ice with ice brooms, while a delicate stone glides slowly on the white ice. In the “Ice Cube”, the curling venue for the Beijing Winter Olympics, a public curling experience competition is underway. Upon closer look, the arena is much more than just a curling arena. It was converted from the "Water Cube", the main aquatics center of the 2008 Beijing Olympic Games, and it is a large-scale project involving the removable, temporary transformation from water to ice.

The Water Cube, which made its mark in the 2008 Beijing Olympics Games, witnessed the glorious moments of many athletes. The social operation of the venue has become a model for the use of Olympic venues after the Games. After Beijing's successful bid for the 2022 Winter Olympics in 2015, a bold idea was proposed to facilitate free water-ice conversion. The venue thus can play a bigger role by providing richer cultural and sports services for the public after the Games. After renovation, the venue will become an important heritage of the city, hosting both the Summer and Winter Olympics Games.

So, how did the "Water Cube" transform into the "Ice Cube"? It should be noted that curling, among all ice events, has the most demanding requirements for the venue. Ensuring the stability of detachable devices is the key problem. After repeated design calculations and tests, the design team finally controlled the margin of error within 2 mm. According to the detachable design of the "Ice Cube", the set ice surface is 8cm thick, which needs repeated pouring of 40 to 50 layers and takes one week to make.

Ice is so "sensitive" that curling venues require no air flow, direct sunlight, or excess heat radiation to be introduced to the ice. To this end, the design team has made intelligent transformations of the ambient temperature, humidity, lighting system and even acoustic system.

The renovated “Ice Cube” can be used for water sports in spring, summer, and autumn and for ice sports in winter. After the Winter Olympics, it will be used for public ice sports training and experience, helping to realize the vision of promoting winter sports among 300 million Chinese people.

Many classic stadiums have been left behind in the century-old history of the modern Olympic Games. They are masterpieces of human engineering architecture and monuments that embody the modern Olympic spirit. However, previous Olympic Games have also faced the problem of the reuse of those venues after the Games. Designers have been seeking new solutions to this problem. For example, after the 1992 Barcelona Olympics, the Olympic village and venues were transformed into tourist destinations. In the 2012 London Olympics, many venues were built with rented building materials for temporary use. Its main stadium “London Bowl” was built with the use of Lego-like structures, and it was rebuilt and leased to West Ham United as its home ground after the Games. In Beijing, from the 2008 Summer Olympics to the 2022 Winter Olympics, from the “Water Cube” to the “Ice Cube”, China introduced the concept of sustainable development into the construction of Olympic venues and explored the comprehensive and lasting utilization, which offers China’s ideas for the development of modern Olympic sports.

生词表

生词

1. 呐喊	nàhǎn	shout loudly
2. 冰壶	bīnghú	curling
3. 拆卸	chāixiè	to dismantle
4. 大放异彩	dàfàng-yìcǎi	show extraordinary talents
5. 荣光	róngguāng	honor, glory
6. 运营	yùnyíng	to operate
7. 典范	diǎnfàn	example, model
8. 限度	xiàndù	limit
9. 严苛	yánkē	harsh
10. 测算	cèsuàn	measure and calculate
11. 误差	wùchā	error
12. 浇筑	jiāozhù	to pour
13. 耗时	hàoshí	be time-consuming
14. 敏感	mǐngǎn	sensitive
15. 热辐射	rèfúshè	thermal radiation
16. 智能化	zhìnénghuà	intelligence
17. 杰作	jiézuò	masterpiece
18. 丰碑	fēngbēi	monument
19. 可持续发展	kěchíxù fāzhǎn	sustainable development

语法点

1. 不仅仅：表示强调。

例句：这个场馆可不仅仅是一个冰壶场馆那么简单。

2. 然而：连词，用在后半句话的开头，表示转折。

例句：经典的奥运场馆建筑是现代奥林匹克精神的丰碑，然而，历届奥运会也都面临着奥运场馆赛后发展的难题。

课文结构分析

请根据这个思维导图，用完整的句子对课文进行复述。

- 冰立方
  - 第一二段 — “冰水转换”工程
    - 水立方
    - 冰立方
  - 第三四段 — 如何变身
    - 可拆卸设计
    - 控制温度、湿度
    - 控制光照和声学系统
  - 第五段 — 场馆使用
    - 春夏秋三季为水
    - 冬季上冰
    - 赛后用于运动培训和体验
  - 第六段 — 场馆赛后发展
    - 可持续发展理念
    - 综合利用
    - 持久利用

练习

1. 根据课文内容选择正确答案。（5 分）

（1）民众冰壶体验赛的场地曾经举办过________。 □

A. 篮球比赛　B. 游泳比赛　C. 跑步比赛　D. 排球比赛

（2）北京在________年成功地申办冬奥会。 □

A. 2008　B. 2015　C. 2022　D. 文章没有提及

（3）冰立方的冰面厚度为________。 □

A. 8 厘米　B. 2 毫米　C. 2 厘米　D. 8 毫米

（4）冰壶场馆一定要做到________。 □

A. 阳光十分充足　B. 空气充分流动

C. 没有直射的阳光　D. 要有微风

（5）冰立方的使用季节为________。 □

A. 春天，冰上运动　B. 夏天，冰上运动

C. 秋天，冰上运动　D. 冬天，冰上运动

2. 根据课文内容回答下面的问题。（5 分）

（1）水立方变身冰立方的设想是哪一年提出来的？

（2）制作冰立方的冰面需要多长时间？

（3）第⑤段中"三亿人上冰雪"是什么意思？

（4）各承办国在奥运会结束后都会遇到什么难题？

（5）从水立方变身到冰立方体现了什么样的理念？

3. 用课文中的词语填空。（5 分）

（1）篮球比赛开始了，大家为队员们________助威。（第①段）

（2）他们的表演肯定会使今晚的活动________。（第②段）

（3）病情可能还会________，要特别小心。（第③段）

（4）有些动物对天气的变化非常________。（第④段）

（5）我们要努力________大自然的奥秘。（第⑥段）

4. 结合课文和网上资料，填写下面的表格。

奥运场馆赛后使用情况一览表

年份	城市	赛后使用情况
1992 年	巴塞罗那	
2000 年	悉尼	
2004 年	雅典	
2008 年	北京	
2012 年	伦敦	

拓展练习

话题活动

观看纪录片《“水立方”是如何变成“冰立方”的？看奥运场馆的华丽变身！》，直观地了解水立方变身冰立方的过程。

话题讨论

以“现代科技是如何潜移默化地影响人们的生活”为主题进行小组讨论，可以考虑科技在教育、交通、医疗、娱乐等领域的应用，也可以扩大自己的思考范围。

写作练习

现在，人们无论在工作中还是在娱乐中都越来越多地使用现代科技，如 AI 或 VR 等。有人认为这会影响人们的想象力和创造力，减少人们的创新精神。你是否同意这个说法？请用 500 ～ 700 字写出你的理由。

文化点

5G 通信

5G 的全称是第五代移动通信技术（5th generation mobile network 或 5th generation wireless technology standard），是最新一代的移动通信技术。自几十年前第一代移动网络技术诞生以来，这项技术已经发生了巨大改变。5G 会比以往任何一代移动通信技术更快、更可靠地传输数据。5G 网络有望实现千兆级的速度，并可将覆盖范围扩展到偏远地区。

5G 的用途十分广泛。在交通运输方面，5G 可以借助实时连接，通过探测驶近的车辆数量来帮助交通信号灯更有效地管理十字路口。在医疗方面，医生可以使用虚拟现实（VR）技术对病人展开远程治疗，人工智能（AI）可以帮助搜寻大量医学数据，帮助医生更快、更准确地进行诊断和制定治疗方案。在农业方面，5G 可以通过引导自动农用设备来提高效率，并操作无人飞机来检测植物健康状况、土壤质量和湿度变化，并精确施用所需的农药、水或肥料。在救援方面，5G 可以更加准确地定位目的地，帮助急救人员更快更确定地提供救援服务。

话题五 对外关系

教学内容和目标	文化点
1. 了解中外友好国家和城市交流往来的故事。 2. 理解中外交流的理念、现状和未来方向。	文明交流互鉴，中国与邻国关系，丝绸之路

课文1　大熊猫

课前热身

请仔细观察下面这张图片，用两分钟左右的时间描述一下你在图片上看到了什么，以及你对图片的理解。

课文 1

扫一扫，看视频

大熊猫

中国很多古籍中都记载过一种神奇的动物，“（它）似熊，小头，痺脚，黑白驳，能舐食铜铁及竹骨”，描述的就是大熊猫。今天看来大熊猫“食铁”是个天大的误会，但也能看出人们对大熊猫实际上是“既熟悉又陌生”的。

“大熊猫”最早被称作“猫熊”。20 世纪是中国新旧文化激荡的时代，新旧书写方式与阅读习惯交杂使用，由右而左书写的“猫熊”被由左而右地读作了“熊猫”。虽然熊猫确实和棕熊、北极熊一样属于熊类，但“熊猫”这一说法却被习惯成自然地流传下来。

别看大熊猫如今混到了濒危动物的行列，然而在进化史上它曾是名副其实的“强者”。大熊猫在地球上生活了 800 多万年，为了适应环境的变化，它们作为一种食肉动物竟然进化出了以竹子为食的习性，为了吃好竹子甚至在熊掌上长出了“大拇指”。强壮如猛犸象、凶猛如剑齿虎都灭绝了，而呆萌的大熊猫却悠然地活了下来。

大熊猫怎么看都是人畜无害的“宝宝”，其实它们的战斗力和呼啸山林的虎豹是一个级别的。大熊猫的咬合力堪比狮子，超过美洲豹，能轻松爬到 10 多米高的树上，在野外山林奔跑时时速能达到 40 公里，是灵活的胖子。

随着人工繁育的难题被陆续攻克，中国人工圈养的大熊猫种群从2002年的161只增加到现在的500多只。人工繁育只是开始，让大熊猫回归野外、实现野外种群的可持续发展才是终极目标。

2003年起，大熊猫开始在野化基地内学习辨认天敌、捕食等野外生存技能，经过科研人员的努力，目前已初见成效。2009年放归野外的大熊猫“泸欣”不仅融入了当地野生种群，拥有了自己的领地，还成功在野外自然配种、顺利产仔。从2010年开始，科研人员采用“母兽带仔”方式进行野化训练，共放归大熊猫12只，其中10只在野外存活。在人类的精心呵护下，大熊猫已经摆脱濒危的境地，不出意外的话，它们将永续繁衍下去。

虽然大熊猫是中国的特有物种，但它们几乎是被全世界人民一起疼爱着的。2017年中芬两国签署了有关熊猫保护的一项协定，一对中国大熊猫被送到芬兰当地的一个自然保护区，受到了芬兰民众的热烈欢迎和热切关注。事实上，作为中国的国宝，大熊猫充当外交使者“旅居”海外已经有很长的历史了。无论到了世界上哪个国家，熊猫都能引起轰动。2018年，四川省政府发起“熊猫与少年”活动，面向全球招募青少年“大熊猫饲养员”。入选的27名全球志愿者在一周时间内与大熊猫亲密接触，体验大熊猫饲养，让全球的“熊猫粉”们羡慕不已。

人们用“看它一眼，就想把全世界都给它”来表达对大熊猫的喜爱。圆滚滚的身材、大大的黑眼圈和憨憨的体态，大熊猫凭借与生俱来的可爱形象在中国的国际交往中发挥着独特的作用，成为最有认知度的中国符号之一。温暖、憨厚、亲切、友善，以及与自然和谐相处的姿态，这些正是中国在国际舞台上展示的形象。

Panda

A mysterious animal is recorded in many ancient Chinese books. "(It) is like a bear, with a small head, feet, and black and white stripes over its body, and can lick and eat copper and iron, as well as bamboo." The strange creature depicted is the giant panda. Of course, believing that giant pandas eat iron is a total misunderstanding, while this subjective idea sheds light on our limited knowledge of the popular animal.

The "Da Xiong Mao" (giant panda) was initially called "Mao Xiong" (panda bear). They made their mark in the twentieth century, an era of conflicting convergence of the new and old Chinese cultures. With the mixing of the old and new reading habits and writing methods, "Mao Xiong", written from right to left, was read from left to right, thus "Xiong Mao" coming into being. While pandas are indeed bears like brown bears and polar bears, the term "Xiong Mao" is habitually passed down.

Even though they are now endangered, giant pandas are strong animals regarding evolutionary adaptability. They were carnivores over eight million years ago, but they evolved into the ones eating bamboo with a thumb in their paw to this end. The chubby giant pandas have survived with a laid-back lifestyle while fierce animals like mammoths and smilodons have perished.

However, don't be fooled by its innocent and harmless appearance; giant pandas can be as fierce as tigers and leopards. Outperforming the jaguar, their bite force is comparable to a lion's. It can easily climb up a tree more than 10 meters high and race in the wild forests at 40 kilometers per hour. Fat as they are, giant pandas are flexible and fast, too.

The number of captive giant pandas in China has increased from 161 in 2002 to more than 500 now, thanks to the development of artificial breeding. However, artificial breeding is only the beginning of a long journey that leads to natural breeding in the wild, ensuring the sustainable development of the precious animal.

Since 2003, giant pandas have begun to learn survival skills such as identifying natural enemies and predation in wild training bases. Efforts paid off. In 2009, the giant panda "Lu Xin" was released into the wild. It has not only become a member of the local wild population, but also has its own territory, mating and giving birth there. Researcher started in 2010 to prepare pandas for life in the wild by training baby pandas on survival skill via their mothers. Twelve giant pandas have been released into the wild, with ten of them alive now. Pandas are no longer on the verge of extinction thanks to the meticulous care from humanity and will sustain their presence on earth.

Although giant pandas are endemic to China, they are almost loved by people all over the world. In 2017, China and Finland signed a treaty on panda protection, according to which a pair of China's pandas were taken to a natural reserve in Finland. This aroused warm welcome and great concern among Finland people. It has been a long time since the panda, as a diplomatic messenger, was introduced overseas. Panda is a hit wherever it goes. Local government in southwest China's Sichuan Province, a major habitat of pandas, launched a global campaign called "Panda and Me" in 2018. The project enrolled 27 young volunteers from around the world to interact with pandas through weeklong activities like breeding, a much-envied short-term job for many panda fans.

People would say they are willing to offer everything to giant pandas out of their love for the cute animal. Pandas are chubby with black eyes and look adorable. Due to its unique role in China's diplomacy, the panda has become an iconic symbol known across the world. Pandas are warm, obedient, kind, amicable, and live in harmony with nature, which are the images China intends to display at the international arena.

生词表

生词

1. 古籍	gǔjí	ancient literature
2. 记载	jìzǎi	to record, to document
3. 舐食	shìshí	lick and eat
4. 文化激荡	wénhuà jīdàng	conflicting cultures
5. 濒危	bīnwēi	be endangered
6. 进化	jìnhuà	to evolve

7. 食肉动物	shíròu dòngwù	carnivore
8. 习性	xíxìng	habit and characteristics
9. 呆萌	dāiméng	adorable
10. 悠然	yōurán	carefree and leisurely
11. 咬合力	yǎohélì	bite force
12. 人工繁育	réngōng fányù	artificial breeding
13. 攻克	gōngkè	to overcome, to resolve
14. 人工圈养	réngōng juànyǎng	artificial captivity
15. 辨认	biànrèn	to identify
16. 呵护	hēhù	take good care of
17. 物种	wùzhǒng	species

成语、俗语、惯用语等

1. 名副其实	míngfùqíshí	be worthy of the name
2. 呼啸山林	hūxiào shānlín	screaming in the woods
3. 初见成效	chūjiàn chéngxiào	achieve initial success
4. 羡慕不已	xiànmù bùyǐ	to envy

语法点

1. 竟然：副词，表示出乎意料，或与预期语境相反。

例句： 为了适应环境的变化，大熊猫竟然进化出了以竹子为食的习性。

2. 怎么……都……：表示强调，强调不管从哪个角度或用什么方法。

例句： 大熊猫怎么看都是个人畜无害的“宝宝”。

3. 无论……都……：表示任何条件下结果或结论都不会改变。

例句： 无论到了哪个国家，熊猫能引起轰动。

课文结构分析

请根据这个思维导图，用完整的句子对课文进行复述。

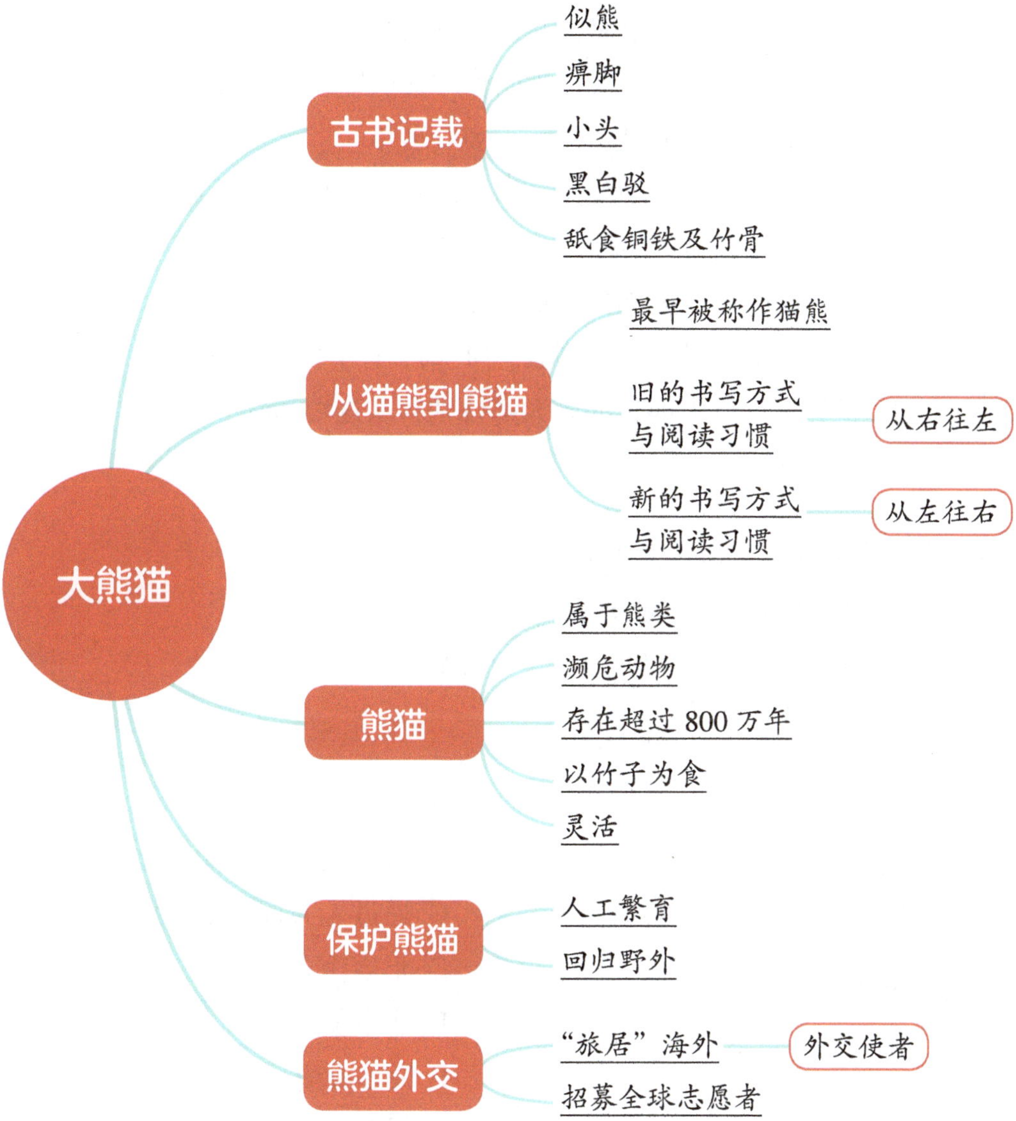

练习

1. 根据课文内容，选出五个正确的表述。（5分）

□ □ □ □ □

A. 今天的大熊猫仍然是能舐食铜铁及竹骨的动物。

B. 大熊猫属于熊类，最早被叫作“猫熊”。

C. 大熊猫在地球上已经生活了800多年。

D. 大熊猫的生活环境变了，所以由食肉动物变成了食竹为主的动物。

E. 温柔的大熊猫其实像虎豹一样凶猛。

F. 2003年开始，大熊猫开始在野外学习辨认天敌。

G. 2009年放归野外的大熊猫“泸欣”有了自己的孩子。

H. 世界上见过大熊猫的人大都特别喜欢这种动物。

2. 根据课文内容回答下面的问题。（5分）

（1）大熊猫的外貌是什么样子的？（2分）

（2）中国旧的书写方式与阅读习惯是怎样的？（1分）

（3）为什么说大熊猫是灵活的胖子？（2分）

3. 根据课文内容，把左边的词语和右边的解释对应起来。（5分）

1. 人工繁育 □
2. 终极目标 □
3. 初见成效 □
4. 轰动 □
5. 羡慕不已 □

A. 同时惊动很多人

B. 最终极端的方向

C. 通过人为饲养令动植物繁衍后代

D. 形容声音大

E. 非常羡慕

F. 最远或最高的理想

G. 开始有效果了

H. 刚开始就能看见效果

课文 2　非洲铁路　中国制造

课前热身

请仔细观察下面这张图片，用两分钟左右的时间描述一下你在图片上看到了什么，以及你对图片的理解。

课文 2

扫一扫，看视频

非洲铁路　中国制造

2016 年 10 月 5 日，“中国制造”的亚吉铁路正式通车。与中国在海外建设的其他铁路项目相比，亚吉铁路不是最长的，120 公里的设计时速也不是最快的，但它却是非洲有史以来第一条电气化铁路。对于内陆国家埃塞俄比亚来说，这意味着它与承载其 90% 以上货物进出的吉布提港的距离从原来的 7 天缩短至不到 10 小时。

早在 20 世纪 70 年代初，中国就已经向非洲兄弟伸出援助之手，修建了东非交通大动脉——坦赞铁路。坦赞铁路从此成为中非友谊史上的丰碑。当时坦赞铁路是由中国政府援建的，40 年后的今天，修建被誉为“新时期的坦赞铁路”的亚吉铁路利用的则是面向全球市场的竞标方式。

这是什么概念呢？谁的实力够强、技术过硬，谁的方案在当地的可行性更佳，谁就能在竞争中胜出。在招标过程中，中国公司的方案和资金支持获得了埃塞俄比亚政府的认可，最终埃塞俄比亚政府选择了与中国企业合作，并用“中国标准”制定了埃塞俄比亚的铁路标准。

亚吉铁路从设计标准到施工、监理，从乘务人员的礼仪、制服到火车票，一切都是纯正的“中国范儿”。这是埃塞俄比亚对中国高铁技术的信任，也是市场化的选择。

亚吉铁路再次让我们看到，中国铁路与非洲的合作大大增强了当地的交通运输能力和互联互通，是“一带一路”倡议的又一个标志性成果。亚吉铁路带动了当地的经贸发展，成为非洲经济增长的新引擎。非洲人民正在享受高铁带来的便利。

African Railway: Made in China

On October 5, 2016, the Addis Ababa-Djibouti Railway, which China built, opened for traffic. Compared with the other projects, this railway is neither the longest nor the fastest, as it is designed to only run at 120 km per hour. However, it is the first electrified railway in Africa, and it provides landlocked Ethiopia with faster access to the Djibouti Port, which ships over 90% of its cargo. The travel time is cut from seven days to less than 10 hours.

As early as the 1970s, China helped Africa to build the Tazara Railway, which links Tanzania and Zambia and is a traffic artery of East Africa. The Tazara Railway has become a monument in the history of Sino-African friendship. However, four decades later, the modern “Tazara Railway” is no longer a project of government assistance, but a business project.

What does this mean? Only countries with advanced technologies and a realistic ability to complete the project were likely to win in the bidding. Ethiopia eventually decided to work with China because of the proposal submitted and the financial support Chinese companies could give. Ethiopia thus established standards for its railways in accordance with Chinese ones.

The Chinese style has been applied to every detail of the Addis Ababa-Djibouti Railway, from its design, construction, and supervision to the etiquette and uniforms of crew members and the design of train tickets. This is a market choice that shows the trust Ethiopia has in China's high-speed railway technologies.

The Addis Ababa-Djibouti Railway once again demonstrates that by cooperating with China Rail, an African country can enjoy a higher traffic capacity and increased interconnectivity. It represents another landmark in implementing the Belt and Road Initiative, boosts the local trade and economy, and provides a new growth engine for the African economy. Moreover, African people are now enjoying the conveniences provided by a high-speed railway.

生词表

生词

1. 援建	yuánjiàn	aid and build
2. 过硬	guòyìng	have a perfect mastery of sth
3. 招标	zhāobiāo	invite tenders (from)
4. 纯正	chúnzhèng	pure
5. 标志性	biāozhìxìng	landmark

课文结构分析

请根据这个思维导图，用完整的句子对课文进行复述。

- 非洲铁路 中国制造
  - 亚吉铁路
    - 通车时间
    - 重要特点
    - 通车意义
  - “新时期的坦赞铁路”
    - 合作模式
    - 纯正“中国范儿”
    - 自主选择
  - 亚吉铁路的影响
    - 加强交通运输能力和互联互通
    - “一带一路”倡议的标志性成果
    - 带动当地经贸发展
    - 非洲经济增长的新引擎
    - 提供便利

练习

1. 根据课文内容判断下列说法的对错，并写出理由。（5 分）

	对	错
（1）亚吉铁路是非洲铁路设计时速最快的。	□	□
理由：________________		
（2）亚吉铁路可以大大缩短内陆到港口的时间。	□	□
理由：________________		
（3）新旧铁路修建的合作模式是相同的。	□	□
理由：________________		

（4）现在非洲国家修建铁路招标时主要看中实力、技术以及可行性。 □ □

理由：____

（5）亚吉铁路带动了当地经济的发展。 □ □

理由：____

2. 用课文中的词语填空。（5 分）

（1）东非交通大动脉坦赞铁路是由中国政府__________的。

（2）基本功__________是他能够在体操比赛中获得冠军的主要因素。

（3）我们公司将会对新项目进行__________。

（4）他操着一口__________的英国伦敦口音。

（5）埃菲尔铁塔是巴黎的__________建筑。

3. 请将左边的段落号码与右边的段意对应起来。（5 分）

（1）第①段 □

（2）第②段 □

（3）第③段 □

（4）第④段 □

（5）第⑤段 □

A. 亚吉铁路的招标过程

B. 亚吉铁路正式通车具有里程碑的意义

C. 亚吉铁路的“中国范儿”

D. 亚吉铁路的盈利前景

E. 与坦赞铁路相比，新时期的铁路有了巨大变化

F. 对亚吉铁路规格参数的详细说明

G. 亚吉铁路的影响力

H. 埃塞俄比亚人民欢迎并喜欢亚吉铁路

拓展练习

话题活动

1. 观看纪录片《熊猫使者》，了解大熊猫在增进中外交流方面发挥的积极作用。

2. 观看《光阴的故事》系列纪录片，了解中外友好交往的历史以及中国人民和世界各国人民之间的深厚友谊。

话题讨论

以“文化交流与全球一体化”为主题进行小组讨论，讨论什么是文化交流，什么是全球一体化，文化交流会否促进全球一体化。

写作练习

在全球化的过程中，人们的生活方式、价值观和意识形态有了更多交流与融合的机会。以“全球化的利与弊”为题目，写一篇 500 ～ 700 字的演讲稿，参加全市的演讲比赛。

文化点

丝绸之路

丝绸之路，简称“丝路”，包括陆上丝绸之路和海上丝绸之路。陆上丝绸之路起自中国古代的长安（现在的陕西西安），经甘肃、新疆，到中亚、西亚，以罗马为终点，全长6440公里。这条路被认为是连结亚欧大陆的古代东西方文明的交汇之路，而丝绸则是最具代表性的货物，因此被称为“丝绸之路”。海上丝绸之路形成于汉武帝时期，当时的海上丝绸之路的主线指的是从中国出发向西航行的南海航线。明代，海上丝绸之路航线进入极盛时期。著名的“郑和七下西洋”是指明朝政府组织的大规模航海活动。这次航海曾到达亚洲、非洲39个国家和地区。随着时代发展，丝绸之路成为古代中国与西方所有政治、经济、文化往来通道的统称。唐代丝绸之路的畅通繁荣进一步促进了东西方思想文化的交流，对以后的世界和民族意识形态发展产生了很多积极、深远的影响。

参考答案

话题一　地理

课文 1　中国的母亲河

1.（1）E （2）C （3）A （4）D （5）B

2.（1）四川省若尔盖县

（2）黄河上游

（3）湿地

（4）河水

3.（1）如痴如醉 （2）凄凉 （3）蔓延

4.（1）拉西瓦灌溉工程

（2）四川省若尔盖县

（3）涂胜

课文 2　澳门

1.（1）B （2）D （3）C （4）C （5）B

2.（1）B （2）H （3）C （4）A （5）E

3.（1）相提并论 （2）中西合璧 （3）触手可及 （4）绚丽迷人

（5）翻天覆地

话题二　人口与民族

课文 1　内蒙古科尔沁草原

1. B　C　D　E　H

2.（1）繁衍生息　（2）辽阔　（3）永恒　（4）虔诚　（5）释放

3.（1）对。理由：牛羊信步，马儿嘶鸣。

（2）对。理由：孕育出科尔沁儿女热情好客、乐观豁达的性格。

（3）错。理由：每逢盛大节日，草原儿女都会穿上华丽的民族服装来到草原上祭祀敖包。

（4）错。理由：在喜庆丰收的日子里、在婚嫁和迎宾的宴会上，人们都要跳安代舞。

（5）错。理由：马头琴是草原上最常见的乐器。

课文 2　新疆大巴扎

1.（1）新疆各地 / 遍布新疆城乡

（2）附近方圆几十里的老百姓都会高高兴兴地前来“赶巴扎”

（3）因为新疆日照充足

（4）贸易的繁盛、丰富的商品，传统手工艺人的技艺代代相传（任选两个）

2.（1）色彩斑斓　（2）琳琅满目　（3）应有尽有　（4）大饱口福

（5）根深叶茂

3.（1）B　（2）A　（3）E　（4）C　（5）G

话题三　教育

课文 1　中国版《放牛班的春天》

1.（1）合唱团。

（2）中文（1 分），英语（1 分），德语（1 分）

（3）想让孩子们走出大山看看外面的世界

（4）名牌大学毕业（1 分），爱好是音乐（1 分）

（5）学生们的乐理为零 / 一点儿都不了解 / 连简谱都不认识

2.A　B　D　E　F　G　J

课文 2　大山里的直播课

1.（1）因为他们的家非常贫困。

（2）网络直播

（3）近千所

（4）可以，因为那里所有的学校都采用统一课表。

（5）促进教育公平

2.（1）F　（2）B　（3）G　（4）C（5）D

3.（1）错。村里条件稍好的家长会把孩子送去外地上更好的学校。

（2）错。一名音乐老师出现在屏幕上。

（3）对。老师们可以通过视频切换跟各教学点的学生互动。

（4）对。促进教育公平是中国政府最看重的民生问题之一，因为它是社会公平的重要基础。

（5）错。鹿马岔小学通过网络直接让贫困学生学习以前接触不到的艺术类课程。

话题四　科技

课文 1　“云游”中国

1.（1）旅游直播

（2）九家

（3）既欣赏了文物（1 分），又增长了见识（1 分）

（4）金顶

2.（1）错。清明前后，正是春游踏青的大好时节。

（2）对。观众在观看直播云游博物馆的过程中，除了能够听到专业、有趣、生动的讲解外，还可通过线上直播平台与讲解员进行互动交流。

（3）错。武汉大学特别开通了“云赏樱”通道。

（4）对。伴随着音乐

（5）对。“云旅游”未来将与景区的线下旅游有机结合。

3.（1）B （2）D （3）F （4）C （5）G

课文 2　冰立方

1.（1）B （2）B （3）A （4）C （5）D

2.（1）2015 年

（2）一周

（3）全国三亿人接触冰上运动

（4）奥运场馆赛后发展的难题

（5）可持续发展

3.（1）呐喊 （2）大放异彩 （3）反复 （4）敏感 （5）探索

话题五　对外关系

课文 1　大熊猫

1.B　D　E　G　H

2.（1）似熊，瘸脚，小头，黑白驳（任何两个）

（2）由右而左

（3）轻松爬到 10 多米高的树上（1 分），在野外山林奔跑时时速能到 40 公里（1 分）

3.（1）C　（2）F　（3）G　（4）A　（5）E

课文 2　非洲铁路　中国制造

1.（1）错。120 公里的设计时速也不是最快的。

（2）对。对于内陆国家埃塞俄比亚来说，这意味着它与承载其 90% 以上货物进出的吉布提港的距离从原来的 7 天缩短至不到 10 小时。

（3）错。亚吉铁路采用的则是面向全球市场的竞标方式。

（4）对。谁的实力够强、技术过硬，谁的方案在当地的可行性更佳，谁就能在竞争中胜出。

（5）对。它带动了当地的经贸发展，成为非洲经济发展的新引擎。

2.（1）援建　（2）过硬　（3）招标　（4）纯正　（5）标志性

3.（1）B　（2）E　（3）A　（4）C　（5）G

出 版 人：王君校
策划编辑：张　超
责任编辑：杨　晗
英文编辑：吴爱俊
封面设计：北京几何创想艺术设计有限公司
排　　版：北京颂煜文化传播有限公司
印刷监制：汪　洋

图书在版编目（CIP）数据

中国文化精读教程 . 当代中国 / 冯薇薇，张超编著 . -- 北京：华语教学出版社，2025.4

ISBN 978-7-5138-2561-0

Ⅰ. ①中… Ⅱ. ①冯… ②张… Ⅲ. ①汉语 – 对外汉语教学 – 教材 Ⅳ. ① H195.4

中国国家版本馆 CIP 数据核字 (2024) 第 032856 号

中国文化精读教程 · 当代中国

冯薇薇　张超　编著

*

华语教学出版社有限责任公司出版
（中国北京百万庄大街 24 号　邮政编码 100037）
电话：(86)10-68320585, 68997826
传真：(86)10-68997826, 68326333
网址：www.sinolingua.com.cn
电子信箱：hyjx@sinolingua.com.cn
北京虎彩文化传播有限公司印刷
2025 年（16 开）第 1 版
2025 年第 1 版第 1 次印刷
ISBN 978-7-5138-2561-0
007900